Aubrey Sampson is a fresh v[...] needs a fresh wind. Lean into these pages and you'll hear the beauty of the Louder Song—that your soul is desperately longing to hear.

> ANN VOSKAMP, *New York Times* bestselling author of *The Broken Way* and *One Thousand Gifts*

There's no denying we live in a fallen, broken, and sinful world—a world of pain—where suffering is a reality for all of us at various levels. Aubrey Sampson peels away the layers of pretense that often masquerade as outward strength or valor as she unpacks an expressive theology of lament. Anchored by her own faith journey and experience of personal loss and suffering, Aubrey encourages authenticity and fosters hope for those who are in the midst of pain and suffering. I am confident this book will be of great encouragement to you as you reflect on the experiences of lament in a world of suffering.

> ED STETZER, PHD, Billy Graham Distinguished Chair of Church, Mission, and Evangelism at Wheaton College and executive director of the Billy Graham Center

If you want permission to ask God the hard questions about suffering, Sampson extends an embossed invitation. Here she offers a highly accessible tour of the lost art of biblical lament, teaching along the way with utmost pastoral care—and with just enough vulnerability to persuade hurting readers that their guide is trustworthy. One certain outcome: You will never look at snow globes the same way again.

> ANDY OLSEN, managing editor of *Christianity Today*

In this vulnerable account of her own pain, Aubrey Sampson helps us believe that life can be hard . . . and God can still be good. Anchored in Scripture and enlivened by storytelling, this powerful book makes something lyrical of lament. And I suppose this, too, is a mystery—that the most beautiful songs are often born out of suffering. *The Louder Song* will be a pleasure to recommend and reread.

JEN MICHEL, author of *Surprised by Paradox*

This is a beautiful book. It is real about lament and honest about suffering, but not without hope. With reflections on lament that are both deeply personal and guided by Scripture, *The Louder Song* composes a harmonious tune that will be restorative music to the ears of anyone who has felt isolated, unknown, or hopeless in their pain. Emily Dickinson once wrote, "'Hope' is the thing with feathers— / That perches in the soul— / And sings the tune without the words— / And never stops—at all—." The buoyancy of enduring, Christ-filled, soul-stirring hope, even in the midst of pain, comes through in Aubrey Sampson's transparent and evocative writing. This is a song you'll want to put on repeat.

BRETT McCRACKEN, senior editor at The Gospel Coalition and author of *Uncomfortable: The Awkward and Essential Challenge of Christian Community*

If you are in the middle of deep hurt, *The Louder Song* is a powerful reminder of how God meets us in the middle of our pain and reminds us we have victory through him. Aubrey's story is a personal lesson in how to pass through disappointment and pain without getting stuck there.

CHRISTINE CAINE, bestselling author and founder of The A21 Campaign and Propel Women

The Louder Song: Listening for Hope in the Midst of Lament is a rare book written with honest, raw emotion about experiencing life's most challenging times. Aubrey Sampson uses stories from her life and Scripture to remind us it's okay to cry out to God when we don't understand. If you're going through a challenging time right now or trying to help someone who is, this book is for you!

> **DAVE FERGUSON**, lead pastor at Community Christian Church, coauthor of *Hero Maker: Five Essential Practices for Leaders to Multiply Leaders*

Having walked through suffering in my own life and with others, I know how tempting it can be to skip right past the hard stuff—and how much we miss out on if we do. In this book, Aubrey Sampson perfectly articulates the beauty of lament and offers it as a gift to anyone who has ever cried out to God—and to the church—in their pain. Through her own story and keen insights, she helps readers learn how to walk through grief while remaining anchored in hope.

> **JAMIE D. ATEN, PhD**, founder and executive director of the Humanitarian Disaster Institute at Wheaton College and author of *A Walking Disaster: What Surviving Katrina and Cancer Taught Me about Faith and Resilience*

If you have ever felt the weight of pain pulling hard at your body and soul—and I know you have—there is solace in these pages. Aubrey teaches us not to hide from pain but to look it in the face, hard and long, and *lament* . . . and, in the depth of this hard, honest song, to find the Louder Song—the presence of the Comforter.

> **CATHERINE McNIEL**, author of *Long Days of Small Things*

A book written from the mind reaches a mind; a book written from the heart reaches a heart; and a book written from a life reaches a life. This book is a life reacher. Aubrey invites us to hold the suffering of life and the sovereignty of God together with both hands.

> TRICIA LOTT WILLIFORD, author of *And Life Comes Back* and *You Can Do This*

What does a person who believes in a good and powerful God do with unimaginable pain . . . and seemingly stone-cold silence from heaven? Aubrey Sampson, from Scripture and experience, says we must lament. Not to find answers, but to "be still in the unanswerable." Not to force God's hand, but to be intimately "tethered to his presence." *The Louder Song* gives hope that in the midst of life-shattering wounds, God sees us and invites us to cry out—raw and real—to him. In response, he comes close, walking with us through our pain, until the day when pain is no more. A must-read!

> KEVIN BUTCHER, author of *Choose and Choose Again: The Brave Act of Returning to God's Love*

I'm celebrating this book on lament. Don't we all need better ways of grieving? Don't we need a better understanding of suffering? Aubrey dives deep into the Scriptures and returns with a biblical map and a voice I shall return to again and again.

> LESLIE LEYLAND FIELDS, editor of *The Wonder Years: 40 Women over 40 on Aging, Faith, Beauty, and Strength*; author of *Crossing the Waters: Following Jesus through the Storms, the Fish, the Doubt, and the Seas*

the

louder

song

Listening

for Hope

in the Midst

of Lament

aubrey sampson

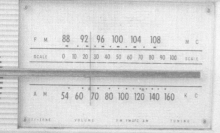

A *NavPress* resource published in alliance
with Tyndale House Publishers, Inc.

NavPress is the publishing ministry of The Navigators, an international Christian organization and leader in personal spiritual development. NavPress is committed to helping people grow spiritually and enjoy lives of meaning and hope through personal and group resources that are biblically rooted, culturally relevant, and highly practical.

For more information, visit www.NavPress.com.
The Louder Song: Listening for Hope in the Midst of Lament

Copyright © 2019 by Aubrey Sampson. All rights reserved.

A NavPress resource published in alliance with Tyndale House Publishers, Inc.

NAVPRESS is a registered trademark of NavPress, The Navigators, Colorado Springs, CO. The NAVPRESS logo is a trademark of NavPress, The Navigators. *TYNDALE* is a registered trademark of Tyndale House Publishers, Inc. Absence of ® in connection with marks of NavPress or other parties does not indicate an absence of registration of those marks.

Cover and interior photographs are the property of their respective coyright holders, and all rights are reserved. Gramophone © George Doyle/Getty Images; radio © ideabug/Getty Images; table © donatas1205/Adobe Stock.

The Team:
Don Pape, Publisher
Caitlyn Carlson, Acquisitions Editor
Elizabeth Symm, Copy Editor
Eva M. Winters, Designer

Published in association with the literary agency D.C. Jacobson & Associates LLC, an Author Management Company. www.dcjacobson.com.

Some of the anecdotal illustrations in this book are true to life and are included with the permission of the persons involved. All other illustrations are composites of real situations, and any resemblance to people living or dead is purely coincidental.

For information about special discounts for bulk purchases, please contact Tyndale House Publishers at csresponse@tyndale.com, or call 1-800-323-9400.

Cataloging-in-Publication Data is Available.

ISBN 978-1-63146-902-2

Printed in the United States of America

25	24	23	22	21	20	19
7	6	5	4	3	2	1

———·◆·———

For Kevin, Eli, Lincoln, and Nolan—

In life's game changes, you have always carried me home.

You are living vavs in times of ekah. Thank you. I love you.

———·◆·———

contents

Be Immanuel inside that sacred, hurting place,
even if it's for only a few precious moments.

MICHAEL CARD, *A Sacred Sorrow*

The weight of this sad time we must obey;

Speak what we feel, not what we ought to say.

WILLIAM SHAKESPEARE, *King Lear*

foreword

As I write this, I'm sitting in a cushioned Starbucks booth in the Charlotte, North Carolina, airport. I've been here before. In this exact spot. About three years ago. And I'm overwhelmed by how much my life has changed in that short span of a thousand days.

I just spent two hours on a plane from Minneapolis, reading Aubrey's words and searching for just the right thing to say to draw *you* into your own lamenting process with Aubrey as your guide. I want to do a bang-up job introducing you to her, because I so believe in the power of Aubrey Sampson's pen! With her scintillating speaking style and her knack for telling an ordinary story in such an extraordinary way, she has certainly made this mentor proud of her, so writing this foreword would be my opportunity to make *her* proud of *me*.

But alas, I walked off the plane and realized my first draft would never work because I wrote it exclusively from my *professional* experience, explaining what I've witnessed as I've escorted *other people* through their painful epiphanies and raw realities. Working with women and couples through their sexual hurts, habits, and hang-ups can provide some pretty rich fodder for writing. But it'd be inauthentic for me to play it safe, stay in my comfort zone, and just write about "other people's problems."

Truth be told, I've done a lot of lamenting of my own the past three years.

I've not wanted to "go there" in my public writings. Not yet. It's felt too fresh, the nerves too raw to dance around them just now. Which is perhaps why I bawled through everything I read on the plane, wiping the constant flow of tears from my eyelashes long enough to focus on one section at a time.

And now here I sit in this cushioned Starbucks booth, where *dread* and *fear* attempt to hold me back, yet *faith* and *hope* propel me forward. It feels bewildering how all of those negative and positive emotions are able to reside together simultaneously, as if "dread/fear" and "faith/hope" are completely unaware of how far apart on the "feel good" spectrum they are, oblivious to their polar-opposite nature. Or maybe that juxtaposition exists only in our minds. Maybe they've actually been intimate friends—no, *close relatives*—all along.

Even through a blurry stream of tears, I can clearly see this connection now. But I wouldn't have recognized it last time I sat here in this cozy booth, because that was *before*—before I faced a major health crisis in 2015, complete with shingles, pinched nerves, shot adrenal glands, and all kinds of stress-induced ailments . . . before my twenty-six-year marriage crumbled into a divorce I never thought would happen to us . . . before my hardworking, hardheaded dad committed suicide on the second day of 2017 . . . before my beloved father-in-law lost his battle with cancer later that spring.

Within a dizzyingly short span of time, I'd lost three of the most important men in my life. Life's landscape kept shifting drastically. One loss after another, a succession of emotional sucker punches to the gut that wouldn't let up long enough for me to catch my breath.

And in case you are wondering—*yes*, I flailed about in all kinds of ways, trying to avoid feeling the full force of it all. (I suspect you probably have with a few flailing tactics of your own.)

I'm still processing, growing, and grieving with intention and purpose. I've learned not to stop—or apologize for—the tears. I've learned to be gentle with myself, accepting the fact that some afternoons, just lying on the couch and staring at the clouds is the only work that really needs to be accomplished. And I've learned that honoring our grievances is much like paying our taxes: They all come due eventually, and the longer we ignore them or attempt to medicate them with our flailings, the more penalties and interest accrue.

As I've reoriented my life around these fresh losses and attempted to press on day by day, well-meaning individuals have often proclaimed, "Oh, your ministry is about to *explode!*" I know they intend this as a compliment or encouragement, but sometimes I just want to scream, "Overwhelming grief is *not* my platform of choice!"

Most of us, if we're honest, would like to choose prettier platforms, lighter loads, easier circumstances, more glamorous roads to travel. We'd like to be the mom whose kids never rebelled even a little bit and who writes about how to live a harmonious family life. Or the fitness instructor who coaches everyone toward looking their absolute best because *she* looks . . . well, you know . . . her absolute best. Or the money guru who's made a killing in the stock market and helps others learn how to invest wisely. Give me *that* kind of platform! But grief? *Good grief!*

Although I have no desire to make moving beyond grief and loss my next platform, I'm oh-so-grateful that Aubrey Sampson has decided to do just that. I've experienced first-hand over the past three years what grief does to a person physically, mentally, emotionally, and spiritually, and I will tell you that none of us should ever attempt to brave this wilderness alone. Regardless of who we are or what other resources we may have access to, we all need to feel a con-nection to a trusted individual who's traveled the path ahead of us and can illuminate our way.

This book is Aubrey's road map for us all—well-crafted because it's been well-traveled. She is no stranger to pain, fear, anxiety, grief, loss, and all that comes part and parcel with these unwelcome intruders. And Aubrey is a guide you can rely on not to leave you in the lurch, stranded somewhere between shock and breathlessness. Her words of wisdom will put air back in your lungs and hope back in your heart.

The Louder Song can truly be just that—a melody above the noise of your grief, drawing your gaze up from the ground in the midst of the curveballs of life. You can stop repressing your pain. As you turn these pages and begin processing and expressing what you're feeling, my prayer for you, dear reader, is that every ounce of dread and fear will organically evolve into deeper-than-ever levels of faith and hope in your life.

Your partner in the journey,
Shannon Ethridge

1
when
your
game is
changed

An Invitation
to Lament and Hope

I SIT ON A BLACK LEATHER COUCH next to my husband, Kevin, in a grief-counselor's office. A box of Kleenex rests on a small coffee table in front of us. One of those framed pieces of coffee-shop art—a black-and-white photograph of rough-hewn hands holding coffee beans—hangs on the wall above us. Coffee and Kleenex, this office seems to say, will solve the world's problems. If only.

We've had a crazy last few years. In 2015, we opened the doors to our church plant, Renewal Church, just as my first book came out. We rejoiced, celebrating some tremendous movement of God in our lives and our neighborhood.

Then—the very same week—I woke up inexplicably unable to walk. I couldn't put any pressure on my legs whatsoever. For days, I scooted around our home like a dog scratching its hindquarters.

Assuming it was a running injury, I tried the old faithful: rest, ice, compression, elevation. No improvement. After a short hospitalization, I was able to walk again, thankfully. But this surprising illness-visitor has evolved into a long-term tenant. I now experience new health issues so disruptive that Kevin has, on more than one occasion, had to carry me around the house. I can't pull tissue from our counselor's box of Kleenex without much effort, let alone hold coffee beans in my palms without experiencing severe pain.

While I suffer from the physical discomfort of this mysterious illness, Kevin suffers too. He made that "in sickness" vow before God and all of our friends and family without really knowing what that might one day entail. Here it is—come to collect. Come to test if we are truly people of our vows.

As if that's not enough, there's also the unresolved search through Crater Lake, Oregon, for a loved one, my cousin and dear friend Cameron. Park rangers find remnants, clues: a coat, broken branches on the side of a cliff, snowshoe prints near a well-traveled photo spot—a place where many hikers before him have gone and returned safely. But not Cam. We hold his funeral in an airport hangar. Photos in lieu of a coffin. Unanswered questions instead of resolution.

And still this: our youngest son's developmental issues. His spinal-cord surgery and ongoing aftercare. His life-threatening allergies. Weeks at Lurie Children's, months of therapy, years where my mama-fears have morphed from molehills into mountains.

And so the bad comes with the good, and it's all a bit too much to manage, contain, or make sense of. It feels like hell and heaven are having coffee together in my kitchen, secretly laughing about some inside joke. But I have no idea what's so funny.

I'd like to tell you that in the face of adversity, I rise above. I overcome. I more-than-conquer. Truthfully, I'm exhausted. And even *that* doesn't feel quite right. Exhaustion implies that at one point there *was* a commodity of energy to be used. And that there is hope for rest again in the future. But with my illness, along with the grief and fear that I currently carry, I can't foresee rest anytime soon. So it's not that I'm exhausted. It's that I'm done, numb, running on empty.

Is this spiritual attack or just my new reality? Life has become this thing I never thought it would. In my youthful naiveté, I believed that hardships were supposed to be the exception to life, not the rule. But suffering is not an exception, after all. It's not a surprise. It's not the interruption to an otherwise easy life. The older I get, the more I realize that no person is untouched by some level of pain and heartache, big or small. Get to know anyone deeply and you'll find their wounds.

Even though I know this fact—that everyone suffers— what's become especially apparent throughout this season is that there's some voice in my head, some combination of pastor/parent/professor/platitude that says I need to handle this suffering and *handle it well*. Learn whatever lesson God is trying to teach me so that I can graduate on to the next stage of spiritual maturity. Be brave. Be strong. Be an example to others. Keep that chin up. Pass the test. Choose joy. Fake it till you make it. Smile.

So I try. I strive. I work excessively to prove how buoyant I can be in the face of adversity.

If a friend is in pain, I can be near her suffering without needing to fix it or clean it up. I'll spend hours listening and crying with her. I'll let her grieve and scream for as long as she needs to. I'm not afraid of sadness. But when it comes to my own pain, for some reason, I've responded differently.

I don't know how to hold these two opposing truths in my hands at the same time: Evil is evil, and God is good and in control over it all. I don't want to admit that I might have to learn to hold God's sovereignty and my own suffering in tension. I don't believe God is the agent of pain, evil, or death. But I don't know how to make sense of God *also* being the one who didn't stop pain, evil, or death from happening to me or those I love.

This is not an ontological argument about God and the existence of evil. I'm a real person, with real faith, wrestling with real pain, in my real-life setting. And it's very difficult. So in these early days of pain, I'm doing everything I can to avoid my conflicting emotions, to avoid reality—to prove how okay and optimistic I am. To keep the spotlight on the Good while ignoring the Bad.

Frankly, it's become absurd. I've become an absurd version of myself. For example, when I'm tempted to feel sad, I'll turn on some upbeat show tunes instead and sing along—loudly. Kevin has heard multiple renditions of "Don't Rain on My Parade" and "A Spoonful of Sugar."

The problem is that no matter how loud I sing, how hard

I try to stay positive, my best efforts at "perky" can't mask the fact that what I really long for are answers, reasons, meaning. Yet even that longing is conflicted and complicated because I also want to pretend that none of this is happening. I want to tie up my pain in a pretty little package. I want to place my suffering in a vacuum-sealed container and hide it under the bed with my skinny jeans and old journals—things I'm desperate to ignore.

But grief won't be contained. Grief won't stay hidden. Grief explodes. Though I know this, I try anyway—try to contain pain with pith. *Every cloud has as silver lining. Everything happens for a reason. Every day with Jesus is sweeter than the day before.* These are things I tell myself and anyone else who will listen. And I keep singing.

"She went full Broadway musical," they'll say in the documentary about my life, just before the scene where they show me going full Grey Gardens.

That's a long way of telling you that Kevin and I should have called the grief therapist when I first started singing smash hits. We probably should have called when, though hounded by grief and illness, I continued to travel across the country to preach, speak, and give life to others; returning a hollow wife and mother, with not much left for my family.

We definitely should've called the therapist when Kevin said, "It's like you're running a marathon with one of your legs cut off, and that's noble and all. But you're expecting me and the boys to run with you, and we're just standing here begging you to stop running altogether. But you can't even hear us. You refuse to listen. Aubrey, we don't want to carry your lifeless body across the finish line."

We finally call the therapist the night that Kevin tries a direct approach, "You're refusing to accept reality. Something has to give. I can't do this anymore."

We have doctors. We have accountability partners. We have close friends in ministry. But we need something more. We need a guide. We need a way through our new season of trial.

So here we are with Mark, the grief and life-change expert. Our thighs sticking to his leather couch, our hands wringing nervously; our shared grief and the coffee-bean art above us, creating an odd sort of cameo.

Mark begins with the dreaded question: "Why have you come in today?"

At which point Kevin passes me the box of Kleenex because at long last, instead of singing, I burst into tears. After a few moments of me blowing my nose, trying to gather my confused thoughts, Kevin senses that if anyone's gonna start this conversation, it has to be him. He scratches his beard and thinks for a moment. "I don't know what to tell you, Mark. The past few years have just . . . they've been a game changer."

I nod in agreement. Kevin's words feel right. Everything is different. Where there wasn't one before, a demarcation exists now, a dividing of my life: before and after. How do I learn to stop pretending and avoiding? How do I learn to exist in this, my new epoch?

The Louder Song

A few appointments later, Mark offers this: "I'd like you to think of suffering as an invitation. You have two choices:

Continue to pretend that it doesn't exist, which clearly isn't working, or accept the offer."

To *accept* comes from the root *to grasp*, to willingly take what is offered.[1] It's the willingness part I wrestle with. I am currently unwilling to take this cup, mostly because I have a lot of questions about it. What precisely does this particular invitation mean? How difficult will it be to accept? I feel a bit like C. S. Lewis, writing to his friend and minister, "We are not necessarily doubting that God will do the best for us; we are wondering how painful the best will turn out to be."[2]

I catch my first glimpse of the answer when a friend invites me to a choir concert. I could use a night out, a night *off* from everything, so I join her.

The performance takes place in this cool little theater-in-the-round in downtown Chicago. As we arrive, ushers pass out programs and point us to our seats. We're running late, so I briefly glance at the program, barely registering the title of tonight's concert. I fold it up and stick it in my purse. We grab our seats just as the lights dim, and a large projector screen descends from the ceiling. The screen flashes a line from Shakespeare's tragedy *King Lear*: "The weight of this sad time we must obey; speak what we feel, not what we ought to say."[3]

Choir members clothed in all black walk onto the stage and start to sing a slow, sad, ancient funeral dirge. Meanwhile, the screen flashes a trigger warning, then cycles through a series of raw images—a starving mother and baby; a child soldier; lands ravaged by famine; high school students participating in a walkout; a funeral; and other visual depictions of pain, poverty, and corruption. The mood in the theater, previously expectant, excited for the concert to begin, soon grows sorrowful and heavy. *Why did we come here tonight?* I think. *This is a mistake.*

What my friend and I don't realize is that while we watch this depressing performance in front of us, a second choir has silently filed into the room and surrounded the entire audience. Quite unexpectedly, they raise their voices and begin to sing over us. It's startling, certainly, but not scary. I immediately recognize their song from my adolescent days, a classic U2 refrain: "I still haven't found what I'm looking for."[4]

As I listen to the familiar words, a thought begins to gently poke and needle at me: *What am I looking for?* Soon, the answer hits hard, sharply. It's a realization about the crux of my struggle, the reason why I've been relentlessly avoiding the reality of suffering.

It's not the pain itself, I realize. It's not even the grief. It's not the fear about what might happen. It certainly *is* those things, but they are coupled with something more, something I haven't wanted to admit. Something I'm terrified to confess, because then it will be real. But this concert, this night won't let me keep it inside anymore.

Here's the truth: I've been looking for God to show up, and he hasn't. Or if he has, I can't seem to find him.

I'm disappointed with God.

He hasn't acted like himself.

He hasn't intervened, or healed, or done what I've assumed he should.

He didn't keep Cameron's feet from stumbling.

He didn't protect my bones from disease.

He didn't prevent my son's struggles.

Where's the healing, the wholeness, the rescue in Jesus that I've been promised?

I've walked with Jesus for so long. We've been through much together. We've overcome together. But now I feel utterly and completely abandoned. I don't know if he will ever calm this storm. I don't know if I will ever find a peace that passes all understanding. Where is God in this? What's he doing? I have no answers for these questions. All I know is that God no longer fits into the box I have designated for him.

I'm trying so hard to fake hope, but I still haven't found what I'm looking for. I'm so afraid I never will. If God never shows up, if he never rescues me, if he never meets me here in this pain, then my entire life of faith—the solid rock upon which I stand—will have been nothing more than quicksand.

Sure, I'm a mature enough Christian to know that when we feel these doubts, we're supposed to choose faith, choose truth, choose hope. Endure. But right now I'm tired of *supposed to*. Tired of pretending to rise above.

In the book of Judges, when the angel of the Lord appeared to Gideon, he pronounced, "The LORD is with you, mighty warrior." You can almost hear Gideon's guffaw in response. *Yeah, right. If God is with us, then why has all this happened to us? Where are God's wonders? Where is his rescue? God is not with us. He has abandoned us.*[5]

I'm here, wanting the same thing Gideon wanted, the thing that every sufferer before me has wanted—proof of incarnation, proof of God's ability, proof of God's power over evil. *God, if you're Immanuel, if you're truly with us, then prove it.*

Unlike Gideon, I can't bear to lay out a fleece or ask for that proof, because I am afraid God will refuse. He'll be offended that I've even dared to ask. What if he doesn't answer? What if he won't show up? Then what will I do? How will I keep going?

"Please do not go away until I come back and bring my offering and set it before you," Gideon pleads with the Lord.

"I will wait until you return," God patiently, lovingly replies.[6]

As I sit listening to these two antithetical choirs in front of me, I plead, silently, along with Gideon. *God, I don't feel strong enough to lay out a fleece, to ask you to show up. But at the very least, please don't go away.*

———•———

Lost in my thoughts, I don't realize that something about the concert in front of me is shifting. I'm not sure I even realize what happens as it does. Maybe it's because I'm familiar with the U2 song, or perhaps it's due to the way the choir has wrapped themselves around the audience like a warm and comforting blanket. They sing like they're performing lifesaving emergency surgery. And somehow the second song begins to overpower the suffering song in front of us. The dirge-choir is still singing. The visceral images are still flashing in front of us. But the hopeful song grows louder. The audience's focus has moved from one song to the other. *I believe in the Kingdom Come. . . . You broke the bonds and you loosed the chains, carried the cross of my shame . . .*

Soon, the choir director invites the audience to sing along with them. My friend and I sit there listening to the rising voices around us. We're crying now, both of us. Almost the entire audience is in tears. We're united by this strange, shared experience. I'm singing and laughing through tears—that emotional cocktail when you feel everything all at once and your body doesn't know which outlet to choose.

At last, I give myself permission to drop the pretending, drop the can-do Mary Poppins spirit. From my gut, my chest, my throat, I let out a deep, loud, guttural sigh, a moan. It's like all of the tidy, tightly coiled pieces of my broken, confused heart finally unfurl and release, exploding all at once. My friend looks at me, shocked. "Are you okay? Do we need to leave?"

"No," I say more forcefully than I mean to, through tears. "We need to stay right here."

For the first time in a long time, I choose to be still. To bear witness to my own suffering and the suffering of others. I don't want to leave. I want to remain present in what feels like a holy, necessary moment.

This concert director has somehow managed to do something I have not been able to do, and I want—*no, I need*—to soak it in. She has artfully acknowledged the existence of evil and suffering without any sugarcoating, without any need to lighten the mood with a show tune, without needing to organize it perfectly on a shelf. She has allowed the unanswerable to remain unanswered while still declaring that suffering will not have the final say.

And then, from someplace sacred and holy, from somewhere deep within the myth inside all of us, I remember that this is what God does.

In a world full of hate, abuse, and game change, God doesn't avoid or ignore pain. He sings a louder song over it. And he invites his hurting people to sing with him.

I reach into my purse and grab the concert program. As

expected, the double-sided sheet of paper contains information about the choir director, the performers, and the songs. But it's the title of tonight's performance I want to read again. It's as simple as it is profound: *A Lament.*

Here at this concert, with Bono's lyrics surrounding me and my friend beside me, I finally understand the invitation of suffering.

Suffering is an invitation to stop pretending.

Suffering is an invitation to stop avoiding.

Suffering is an invitation to let go of control.

Suffering is an invitation to pour out our hearts.

Suffering is an invitation to lament to God.

What Is Lament?

For those of us who follow Jesus, we live with down payments on the "Already" of God's Kingdom on earth. We see glimpses of God's healing power, his love, and his victory over evil. But we also live in the "Not Yet" of a broken, sinful world.

It is in between the Already and the Not Yet that we wait expectantly for the return of Jesus, who will one day make all things right, whole, and complete. Thankfully, we experience glimpses of gospel hope every time we see bits and pieces of God's reign and presence and power at work. But that final redemption—God's Kingdom arriving in full, all brokenness redeemed, all evil thwarted, all suffering ended—is our ultimate hope.

Lament, a crying out of the soul, creates a pathway between the Already and the Not Yet. Lament minds the gap between current hopelessness and coming hope. Lament anticipates new creation but *also* acknowledges the painful reality of now. Lament helps us hold on to God's goodness while battling evil's evil at the same time.

Lament is an overlooked genre of prayer found all throughout Scripture. There are actually more lament songs than praise songs in the Bible. The Psalms alone contain more than sixty-five laments, including laments for fallen warriors, for illnesses, for victims of suffering, for the dead, and more. There are laments of vengeance, protest, repentance, loss, and even depression. Beyond the Psalms, the Scriptures also include words from famous lamenters like Rachel, Hannah, Moses, Job, Tamar, Jeremiah, and of course, Jesus. God gives us the laments of those who have gone before us as a way to talk honestly with him, as a way to enter into the biblical story, as a way to connect with the suffering people of God, and as a tool for thrusting our anger and our mysteries and our losses at him.

Even though laments fill the pages of our Bibles, for most Western evangelicals and post-evangelicals, lament prayers remain unfamiliar, mostly absent from our church calendars, conferences, and small-group curriculums. But lament is actually a godly concept, a spiritual discipline, and a powerful handhold in our seasons of sorrow. God has given us the biblical language and practice of lament as a way to express our pain and survive our suffering.

When the days are hard—when grief weighs as much as gravity, when we can't live a minute longer with the pain, when we're angrier or more disillusioned than we ever thought possible, when we can't find the right words for our difficult emotions, when our gnawing questions become too much to handle—my prayer is that God's Spirit will draw us back, time and time again, to lament, and ultimately into his presence.

And this is how, somehow, even in our darkest, most grievous laments, there's hope—because we don't lament to a void. We lament to the God who *wants* our laments. As we lament, we join in the chorus of those who have gone before us—those who have wrestled with suffering's reality and come out, not unscathed, but still proclaiming God's goodness.

Lament can lead us back to a place of hope—not because lamenting *does* anything magical, but because God sings a louder song than suffering ever could, a song of resurrection, renewal, restoration, and *re*-creation. Lament helps us to listen for God's louder song and to believe that one day, we will hear it above the noise of our pain.

The Invitation

After the concert, I return home to a quiet house. Kevin and the boys are all tucked in and sound asleep. Taking advantage of the stillness and the emotion of the concert, I don't go straight to bed; I want the chance to think over my therapist's question again. Can I accept the invitation of suffering?

I understand now what the invitation is. In our pain, God invites us to express our grief about the unraveling of life. At the same time, we are invited to unabashedly, unashamedly declare that we want it back. No more Broadway musicals, no more pretending. Just the naked self, standing before

God—all of our disappointments, deferred dreams, and disillusions in tow.

I don't play any instruments, so I can't strum a U2 ballad. Even if I wanted to write a song, I don't have the right words to express the weight of my pain. Instead, I open my Bible to the poetry of the Creation story, to find some words to lean on.

I grab my journal and pen and write a prayer, a shaky attempt at lament. For the first time, I'm ready to acknowledge how hurt I actually am. And though it's certainly not a finished lament, this feels like a good start.

Father God, the Eden you and I have existed in for some time seems to be crumbling before my very eyes. You're not walking with me or I'm not walking with you—I can't tell which anymore. I feel naked and ashamed, vulnerable. Chaos has ensued. Darkness hovers here. My world is formless and void. Do you see me? My family? My marriage? My children? Can you hear our cries? Creator God, please create again. Maker of heaven and earth, remake this brokenness into something new, something better. Help me hear you, help me listen for hope. Help me endure.

A Lament by Job

At this, Job got up and tore his robe and shaved his head. Then he fell to the ground in worship and said:

"Naked I came from my mother's womb,
    and naked I will depart.
The LORD gave and the LORD has taken away;
    may the name of the LORD be praised."

In all this, Job did not sin by charging God
with wrongdoing.

JOB 1:20-22

how

Ashley's Lament

ASHLEY IS ONE OF MY KIDS' favorite babysitters. One summer, she watched them nearly every day so I could finish writing my first book. My sons and I learned a lot from this strong young woman as she watched her older brother battle cancer. The first funeral my sons ever attended was his.

Ashley shared this lament with me and gave me permission to share it with you. If you grieve, may you find a kindred spirit in Ashley and sense the love in her lament.

Ashley

If you had asked me as a young girl to talk about pain, I would have told you that *pain* is a word associated with the physical: skinning your knee, getting a shot, snagging your arm on a branch while tree climbing.

I was very active as a child, which, of course, led to me getting hurt. A lot. Such as one afternoon when I was riding my bike with some neighborhood kids. I don't remember the fall, just my arm stinging a little. What I do remember most vividly is my friends' reactions.

Taylor's eyes went wide with horror. Dustin ran straight home. Riley told me that we were finished playing, that I needed to leave my bike and get home as fast as I could. We had never played like we were delicate china dolls, but suddenly I was so fragile in their eyes.

I went home with my head down, annoyed that I was wasting prime afternoon play hours. When I walked through our front door, I yelled for my dad, told him I'd fallen and my friends had sent me home. When he walked around the corner and saw me, he immediately froze. He turned a shade paler and tried not to gag. What I assumed was just a little scrape was actually a shredded forearm. When my dad ushered me to the bathroom sink to wash me off, I finally understood the seriousness of the damage.

My father carefully held my arm and started to pick out the blacktop bits. That's when I saw my little seven-year-old frame in the mirror, bloody and helpless, and the fear in my dad's face. By then, the initial adrenaline was wearing off and the awareness of pain had set in. I started crying and looked in the mirror again. It dawned on me that I wasn't some cool biker chick. I was just a seven-year-old girl who had been riding her bike a little too wildly, and I got hurt, simple as that. But that was pain.

Physical pain as a young child is one thing, but when you see it, as an adult, in another's eyes, when you see it in their actions, when you're scared for someone you love—that type of pain is completely indescribable.

Thirteen years later, I took up my father's position as a caretaker. But this time, I stood by my dad and the rest of our family as we tended to my eldest brother, who was only twenty-four at the time, after he was diagnosed with rhabdomyosarcoma, a rare, aggressive pediatric cancer. He was living in Vancouver, and after a chest X-ray at the ER for a bad cough, a nurse flippantly told him that it looked like he had a large mass in his chest and that it was probably cancer. (Let's just say, I've learned the importance of bedside manners.)

The doctors in Vancouver told my brother that his tumor was inoperable and incurable, and that he had only a few months to live. There was no second opinion.

When I got the phone call, my insides felt as demolished

as my little arm did after that rugged bike injury. I was driving to a friend's house, and I remember turning up the car radio loud enough to prevent my mind from thinking. I wouldn't let myself cry. I couldn't be in pain because this couldn't be real.

To see your playmate, a brother you love so dearly, suffer feels like holding an important secret that no one else in the world can know. Most people say that it's better to be strong in the face of a loved one's suffering; that it's not fair to be hurting when we're not the ones in a hospital bed. But my heart felt more and more wrung out every day.

I prayed so many times that God would remove all cancer cells from my brother. I prayed that I might be inflicted with the disease so that he could have his life back. *Why did it have to be him? How will we get through this?*

Though this is the biggest valley my family has ever trudged through, God's hand is evident in it. Many people have prayed for us. They've donated money and food. They've offered to paint our house, watch our dog, and plan birthday parties for us. Some friends even arranged a trip for our family of six to travel to Hawaii.

My brother's life was a daily battle until the end. We are still grieving. We will always grieve. Still, I will choose to worship and follow God, especially in this pain. I will know him here, as much as I know him in my pleasure. I will hope in Revelation 21:4: "'He will wipe every tear from their eyes. There will be no more death' or mourning or crying or pain, for the old order of things has passed away.")

2

it's
okay
to be
honest

OUR YOUNGEST SON, Nolan, has to recuperate from spinal-cord surgery flat on his back, gently strapped to a Kangaroo Board. That, or we throw our legs over him and do our best to keep him entertained with stories and silly faces. It's all-consuming and counterintuitive to keep a little boy from rolling, playing, or crawling—doing all the things a baby should do—for months.

Thankfully, we have help. Nolan has an amazing team of heroes around him—his neurosurgeon and physical, occupational, and speech therapists—all of whom drive to our home or see us at their offices regularly. We know this isn't the case for all families, and we recognize that we are privileged in this, his health care. Still, when Nolan turns two—well over a year postsurgery—his recovery remains arduous. His ongoing physical development dawdles.

We learn to celebrate small victories. The first time he says the word *bath* and the day he finally steps up the stairs rather than crawls. By the time the kid turns five, he talks incessantly and climbs constantly, but we can't see the future. At two, the word *bath* feels like a baptism—the steps up stairs, his wedding day.

After a couple of years of Nolan's steady diet of care, we need a break. So Kevin, the boys, and I escape from our home in Chicago to a family member's lake house in Oklahoma. Nolan is thankfully moving very well now. He's like a souped-up engine that's been stuck in idle far too long. Nolan rockets into his newfound freedom with excitable energy and vivacious curiosity, especially here at the lake. He is passionate about exploring the shore with his big brothers, throwing pebbles into the water, and fishing. I'm filled with wonder and gratitude for every step, every splash, every release of the reel. All of it means Nolan is growing stronger.

One morning of our vacation, I wake up and can't find my little explorer anywhere. When I notice that his kid-sized fishing pole is missing, I know immediately in my heart, in my skin, in my entire being where he's gone. He left the lake house to fish at his favorite spot—out on the docks over the water.

In an instant, I become lightning, a mom-version of the Flash. I bolt out the door—shoeless, still in my pajamas, screaming his name. I trip; my legs can't keep up with my emotion. When I finally make it to the bridge, to the little overpass that leads to the boat docks, I imagine the worst.

Mercifully, I find quick and sweet reprieve. An older gentleman is walking toward me, carrying a crying Nolan in his arms. I mutter a curse word and a praise in one breath out of pure relief. This man doesn't even have to question my relationship to Nolan. He knows by the pale panic on my face, by the agony of my soul, by my tears, that *Mommy has arrived.*

I grab Nolan from this stranger's arms while thanking him profusely. Then I sprint to concrete, to solid ground, to as far away from water as possible. I drop to my knees and hold Nolan closer than I have held him before, closer than I did the night of his surgery. I sob. Nolan sobs. I tell him over and over that I love him. I rock him. If I could have done so, I would have tethered us together with a permanent rope, so he'd never wander again.

In the middle of our communal tears, my mood drastically shifts. I grab Nolan hard by the arms. I look him directly in the eyes and speak sternly: "You may never, *ever* go to the water without Mommy or Daddy. Do you understand me? You may never do that again."

Nolan, scared by my intensity, thinks he's in trouble and starts to cry again. I don't mean to scare him, but I want him to understand. I need him to know what could have been. Years later, Nolan still remembers the day he went to the lake alone. The day the stranger rescued him.

And now, in this difficult season, I remember it too. This is what this *stuff*—this grief, sorrow, sickness, fear—feels like. I'm running on jellyfish legs in some frenzied direction, desperate to get there but also terrified of what I might find when I arrive. I need a rescuer.

I'm waiting for God to step in and save the day. But for the first time in my thirty-year Christian faith, I'm struggling to believe that God even sees me here. And yet, I also know that if I am going to make it through, I can't keep my anger and frustration and intense emotions bottled up any longer.

Oftentimes our biggest obstacle to lament (besides not knowing enough about it) is that we don't know if it's okay to complain to God. We're told by Paul to "rejoice in the Lord always." He even says it twice just in case we missed it the first time, "Rejoice!" (Philippians 4:4). How do we follow that command and simultaneously lament? How do we praise God *and* complain to God (sometimes about God) without offending him?

Let's say that I told you that in almost two decades of marriage, Kevin and I have eagerly agreed with each other's every decision and whim. We've never experienced conflict or even conflict resolution! We never confide in one another about what upsets, hurts, or saddens us, because that might ruffle the other person's feathers. It might offend or push them away. What would you say to that description of marriage?

You'd probably laugh in my face. And I'd deserve it. Even if you aren't married, we all know that any relationship built *solely* on positivity, praise, and shallow conversation is not actually an intimate relationship. It might be fun for a time. But it wouldn't be realistic. Nor would it be a safe place to express deeper or even painful emotion. It would be a marriage where neither partner had a true, whole voice, where neither partner was sharpened or growing in maturity.

Or to make things a little more extreme, what if I told you that only one of us had a voice in the marriage? That only one of us shared our deepest feelings and thoughts and wounds while the other remained completely silent and passive, uninvolved? What kind of relationship would that be? Certainly not a healthy, whole one.

True lament can only happen in the confines of a safe, loving covenantal relationship, whereby we are free to be our truest selves without fear that our partner will walk away or stop loving us. "It is an illusion to suppose or postulate that there could be a relationship with God in which there was only praise and never lamentation," writes theologian Claus Westermann. "Just as joy and sorrow in alternation are part of the human existence (Gen 2–3), so praise and lamentation are part of [our] relationship to God."[1]

In other words, we don't have to fear expressing the whole gamut of emotions to God, because that is part of a covenantal relationship with him. Even if we turn our prayers against him, even if we angrily blame him, even if we run and scream wildly, God remains near, patiently inviting us deeper into his presence. When Christians lament, we do so to a God who lets us. Our cries—even our cries of doubt and despair—fall on his loving, listening ears.

What's remarkable about Christianity is that we have a King who is also a steadfast, loving Husband and Friend. He not only permits lament; he *gives us the language* of lament. We have a God who desires and deserves our wholehearted praise. But he is also a God who wants an authentic, meaningful, intimate love relationship with us. We have a groom who gives his bride a voice.

25

Even if our lament is impolite, raw, or bitter, even if we express sorrow or verbalize anger, even if we make demands, as we lament, we actually preach to the world (and to ourselves) that it is possible to have a fearless, deeply intimate relationship with God. A God who not only is worthy of our thanksgiving and our joyful worship but *also* wants every part of us—not just our "pretty" selves, but our sharp edges, our sin struggles, our suffering, and our sadness.

If we never acknowledge our pain to God, we will never truly know what it means to praise him on the other side of suffering. It is in our honest crying out *to God* about our pain that our worship *of God* grows more authentic. It is in this kind of relationship, this kind of honesty with God, that our walks with him become real. Lament is part of the rhythm of a deepening relationship with him.

Still, if and when we begin to feel comfortable expressing our more honest emotions to God, questions still remain: How exactly *do* we lament? What does it look like? How do we think about it and understand it, theologically and biblically?

Expressions of Lament

If you've been in a season of pain, you know that grief can take any number of forms. You may express your grief on the phone with an old friend, sharing memories and laughter. You may scream or sob in the privacy of your bedroom or shower. Perhaps you need to experience the stillness of nature or the silence of winter in order to help you find the right metaphor for your pain. Grief is dynamic in that way, ever-shifting.

Like grief, lament can also emerge through a variety of mediums and expressions. Lament, an articulation of pain and sorrow, can be communicated through poetry, prose, protests, and prayer. Modern adaptations of lament show up in films, works of art, songs, and even hashtags. Lament is usually expressed verbally or visually and can be personal or communal, even national.

As we think through what lament looks like for us, we can find our best insight in God's Word. Lament, above all, is a dialogue between us and God, and he has given us a beautiful picture of what that looks like throughout Scripture. Let's explore four expressions that I've found especially meaningful in my own journey: the Shalom lament, the Exodus lament, the Protest lament, and the Repentant lament.

The Shalom Lament

Some scholars talk about how the earliest lament emerged from the ground, as the blood of the murdered Abel cried out to God.[2] But I believe lament began in the Garden of Eden when the juice of sin's forbidden fruit dripped down Eve's and Adam's chins. Lament started when sin entered and marred God's *very good* world.[3]

Though we know that God is always good, life doesn't always feel that way. In fact, all biblical lamenters from Jeremiah to Jesus respond to a sensation of God's absence. They lament, as we do, when God's shalom—his peace, blessing, well-being, wholeness, relational justice, and Kingdom come—seems to have disappeared. Ultimately, all laments are reactions to the absence of God's shalom.

In the Creation narrative of Genesis 1, God made the heavens and the earth. But he soon saw that the earth was dark, formless, chaotic, and empty. I sometimes wonder if *this* was the actual first lament, when the earth itself was void of shalom. Things weren't robust and splendid. So God responded to the earth's own lament by adding more of his goodness. He lit up the dark sky with stars and sunlight.

God saw that the ground was dry and brittle, and that wasn't good either. So he countered by pouring out raindrops and dewdrops and ocean tides. He separated waterfalls from water-filled skies. Again God noticed that the land was barren; the land itself lamented. So God created sweet, juicy strawberries and sky-colored blueberries, as well as honey, milk, coffee beans, and butternut squash.

Soon God realized that without seasons, his people would stay stuck in disarray. Our lives would waste away in confusion. So God created a beautiful order to nature—snowflakes and spring daffodils, summer rain, and the reds and golds of fall.

Then God heard another lament—man's loneliness. Adam needed an equal partner in war, in life, in love, in work, in creativity, and in enjoyment. Isolation had to change; emptiness could not remain. So God created bone of Adam's bone, flesh of his flesh: Eve.

This is what God does. More than that, this is who he is. Into our dark night, he brings stars. Into our drought, he brings water. Into our pain, he brings friends and family. From our misery, God makes meaning. He transforms our pain into purpose and our suffering into splendor. He transforms our *not good* into his *very good*.

Usually a source of great encouragement and hope, this *very good* aspect of God's character can sometimes cause our faith to feel fragile and tenuous, especially in times of grief and loss. These suffering seasons can make us question why God is not doing what he is supposed to do. Why isn't God being who he's revealed himself to be—a creator of beauty; a supplier of light; a bringer of order and wholeness, peace and goodness?

What do we do when we keenly sense the absence of God's hand, the lack of his shalom? How do we respond to another senseless death? Another month with an empty womb? Another week wondering if we'll ever have a healthy, loving relationship? Another failure at work? Another day of unemployment? Another diagnosis? Another heartache? Another regret? Another sin struggle? Another no? Another financial stressor? Another hurting child? Another broken relationship?

That's when we have to learn to lean into our lament muscles, to speak the weight of this sad time, to declare to God the absence of his shalom and remind him of the prom-ises of his wholeness and newness. To lament is to speak the reality of our formless, chaotic suffering and to ask God to fill it with his *very good*.

Lament says, "God, you have described yourself as one thing, but my life, my community, and my city currently reveal something totally different. Please! Help me see your hand in this. You broke the power of evil on the cross and at your resurrection—so be victorious again! Show me your goodness again."

To lament is to long for the shalom of God, no longer in

part but in whole. It is a cry for the promise of Revelation 21:3-4, that "God's dwelling place [will be] now among the people, and he will dwell with them. They will be his people, and God himself will be with them and be their God. 'He will wipe every tear from their eyes. There will be no more death' or mourning or crying or pain, for the old order of things has passed away."

The Exodus Lament

If you read the Old Testament, you will see that laments are at the heart of the relationship between God and his people. Over and over, as God's people encountered trouble and trial, and as they faced their own idolatry and sin, they cried out (lamented) to God. We see this especially in the Exodus.[4]

The story of Exodus begins with the oppression, enslavement, and infanticide of God's people. And during that long period, the people's despair found voice in laments to God. Exodus 2 tells us that "God heard their groaning and he remembered his covenant with Abraham, with Isaac and with Jacob. So God looked on the Israelites and was concerned about them" (2:24-25). The word *concerned* in Hebrew is a verb (*yada*) that describes God's intimate knowing of his people.[5] It is even used at times to describe sexual relationships. God is intimately intertwined with the suffering of his people. He sees them. He hears them. He knows them. He is moved with compassion to rescue them.

It's worth mentioning that even before the Israelites cried out, God had already initiated his rescue plan through Moses. God's salvific action wasn't dependent on the prayers of his people. His perfectly orchestrated rescue operation was already in motion. But there is something significant that Exodus seems to tell us about the cries of God's people: Our laments stir the heart of God.

I love my three sons, always. I am constantly on the lookout for ways to protect them, provide for them, teach them, disciple them, and mother them well. But when my boys get emotional—when they express their pain to me, when they cry, when they want me to hold them and be near them—that stirs my heart. Their articulation of sadness awakens my emotions toward them. You better believe that when Nolan was crying before his surgery, my affection, adoration, and feelings about him were intensified. It's not that my love for Nolan ever changed, but the current of my emotions did. Such is God's parental love for you.

God's love doesn't advance or retreat based on our efforts or work or words. But our laments, our crying out of pain, certainly appeal to God's parental heart, his abundant love, the riches of his mercy and grace. Think about that for a moment: Your emotions touch the compassionate heart of God.

Back to Exodus. Upon hearing the anguish of the Israelites, God unveiled his plan for their rescue and freedom. The Lord used Moses to display his great power against the tyrannical, evil Pharaoh and delivered his people from their oppression. Exodus 14 tells us that, after being rescued by the lamb's blood at Passover and after walking through the opened waters of the Red Sea, God's people put their trust in their Lord again.

The book of Exodus begins with a lament story. Chapter 15 ends with songs from both Moses and his (and

Aaron's) sister, Miriam. "Sing to the LORD," they cry out with the other Israelites, "for he is highly exalted. Both horse and driver he has hurled into the sea." Moses' song includes this beautiful verse as well: "The LORD is my strength and my defense [in older translations, *my song*]; he has become my salvation. He is my God, and I will praise him, my father's God, and I will exalt him."[6]

Every lament is an Exodus journey. In fact, most biblical laments follow the pattern of the Exodus: The lamenter suffers; the lamenter expresses that suffering to God; God responds with compassion; God hears, sees, delivers. In time, the lamenter is transformed and puts his or her hope again in God.

Psalm 10 contains a beautiful example of an Exodus lament: "Why, LORD, do you stand far off? Why do you hide yourself in times of trouble? . . . But you, God, see the trouble of the afflicted; you consider their grief and take it in hand. The victims commit themselves to you; you are the helper of the fatherless" (1, 14).

When we lament like the psalmist above, we also relive an Exodus journey—both in the expression of our laments and in the living of them. We suffer. We declare our suffering to God. We ask him to see us. The painful part is not knowing how long we will walk through the suffering. How long until we arrive at the dry shore and sing our songs of praise?

In time, though, we recall that God delivers. We remember our salvation by his blood and our baptismal identity in the waters. We recall his powerful rescue and help in our lives. As the lamenter is changed by God, so is his or her lament.

The Protest Lament

Our church plant recently gathered with a few other churches in our city for a night of candlelit lament for the DREAMers in our city. We cried out to God to have mercy on these children and to change policies. We followed up with action—tweeting, writing, and calling our local and national leaders.

Lament expresses grief for our own pain, of course. But it is also a communal and public cry for justice. Folk musicians, hip-hop artists, and peaceful resisters like Dorothy Day and Martin Luther King Jr. understood this. Viral hashtags about inequality embrace this kind of lament.

Protest laments cry out to the only judge who can actually make a difference and demand a just ruling from him. These laments express outrage, sorrow, and repentance for communal sin such as racism, violence, blind triumphalism, school shootings, sexism, and more. Protest laments give voice to evil, inequitable, and unjust power structures and demand a redistribution of that power. They are "as dangerous as Lech Walesa or Rosa Parks asserting with their bodies that the system has broken down and will not be honored any longer."[7]

The book of Lamentations, which we will look at a bit more throughout this book, is a prime example of Protest lament. Jeremiah cries out on behalf of his despairing nation, "I called on your name, LORD, from the depths of the pit. You heard my plea: 'Do not close your ears to my cry for relief.' You came near when I called you, and you said, 'Do not fear.' You, Lord, took up my case; you redeemed my life. LORD, you have seen the wrong done to me. Uphold my cause!" (Lamentations 3:55-59). Jeremiah demands that

God, the judge, hear his case, take up his cause, and declare a better verdict than the anguish he currently sees.

I personally believe Protest laments are one of our most powerful ministry and evangelistic tools, because these laments actually give dignity to the marginalized sufferer. They take someone's suffering seriously. They allow us to earn relational credit with those who are hurting—and in so doing, we can share the love of Jesus. Protest laments say, *We will not brush aside the pain that you or your people are experiencing or ignore your plight any longer. We will intercede for you at the throne room of God. We will demand change from the God who can do something about it. We will bear your suffering as if it were our own. We will repent from any pain we have caused, or any sinful wrongdoing in which we have participated. We will own our part in injustice. We will love you in this way and show you that you are loved by God and that Jesus' Kingdom is real.*

The Repentant Lament

A professor of mine who lived in Romania for a time said that Christians there were known as "The Repenters." I love that. Our lives should look different from the rest of the world because we are followers of Jesus, and we have committed to follow the way of Jesus through repentance. We have vowed to make sure he is not the supporting character in our stories, but the lead, the boss, the King. Turning to Jesus is not a onetime thing; we return to him again and again and again.

We will make mistakes as we follow him. We will forget to die to ourselves. We will bow down to idols of our own making. But to be a Christian means that we will allow the Lord in his kindness to draw us back to repentance and obedience time and time again.

Our Repentant laments express just that—remorse for sin and a desire to return to the Lord. Amos did this when he prophesied about his people's sin, calling them to Repentant lament: "Go out into the streets and lament loudly! Fill the malls and shops with cries of doom! Weep loudly, 'Not me! Not us, Not now!' Empty offices, stores, factories, workplaces. Enlist everyone in the general lament. I want to hear it loud and clear."[8]

Another famous Repentant lament came from the mouth of Isaiah. When the prophet saw the Lord high and exalted, his only response was lament: "Woe to me! . . . I am ruined! For I am a man of unclean lips, and I live among a people of unclean lips, and my eyes have seen the King, the LORD Almighty" (6:5).

Isaiah's lament communicates a profound aspect of our relationship with God. When we are faced with God's holiness—when we consider his sacrifice, his grace, his love, and his rule—we can't help but be humbled by our own sin and our desperate need for his salvation.

But thanks be to God, by the Spirit, we are reminded of the truth of the gospel again and again, just as Isaiah was reminded: Our guilt has been taken away by the blood of the Lamb and our sin has been atoned for (6:7). Our laments for sin can transform into repentance—and eventually into songs of praise and obedience. ("Here am I. Send me!"[9])

We can also lament for the sins of others (though we cannot repent for them). In fact, many (if not all) of the Old Testament prophets were lamenting for the sins of their nation.

The seventeenth-century Puritan minister Thomas Watson, in his essay *A Divine Cordial* (first published in 1663) wrote about the "good" of lament for the sin of others: "God's people weep for what they cannot reform. 'Rivers of tears run down mine eyes because they keep not thy law (Psalm 119:136).' David was a mourner for the sins of the times; his heart was turned into a spring and his eyes into rivers. Wicked men make merry with sin. . . . But the godly are weeping doves."[10]

The godly are weeping doves. What a lovely image—it contains sorrow for sin and the shalom of Christ, all at once. As followers of Jesus, we are people of both—the cross *and* the Kingdom. We know Christ and his sufferings but we also know the victory of his resurrection. Therefore our laments should reflect it all—regret *and* return to the Lord.

Come Near

No matter what form lament takes in Scripture, we see over and over that our God aligns himself with suffering people. Just look at Jesus, Man of Sorrows, who publicly lamented over the death of his friend Lazarus. He lamented over the city and the people of Jerusalem. He lamented on the cross. He lamented for his own pain and for us. He pulled his dear friends aside in the garden of Gethsemane and said, "My soul is overwhelmed with sorrow to the point of death. Stay here and keep watch with me." Then he fell, his face on the ground, and lamented again: "My Father, if it is possible, may this cup be taken from me. Yet not as I will, but as you will."[11]

Jesus knew lament intimately. In fact, Jesus did one better; he *became* lament for us—he took our laments on himself on the cross. Because he knows suffering personally, Jesus is not afraid of our honest expressions of pain. In Jesus, our suffering can become a place in which God bids us, "Come near."

Come to me in your pain. Express it to me, child. Allow me to show you my compassion. Dive deeper into intimacy with me until your sorrow turns back into praise. Like I did at Creation, like I did in the Exodus, like I have done in my courts, like I did on the cross—through my suffering and in your suffering, I will show up. I will rescue you. I will display my very good *once more.*

———•◦•———

As I sit on the concrete pavement near the lake, with Nolan still wrapped tightly in my arms, I am certainly not thinking just yet about the various expressions of lament. I don't know or frankly care about these things. I just know that I want to learn how to speak my pain to God, to say the words of my disappointment. But I still have a ways to go.

As you begin to think about your own lament, you don't need to know all of the theological and biblical ramifications of it. All you really need to know for now is this: When the only thing you can sense is God's absence, lament is the rope that will keep you tethered to his presence. Lament helps you hold on to God because it is an honest form of worship and communication with him. If you can't find your own lament words for now, that's okay. Begin by searching through the Bible. Read—maybe even pray aloud—the words of the ancient Shalom, Exodus, Protest, and Repentant lamenters.

In time, I hope you'll run wildly toward God, your own

unedited, honest laments in hand. May you find him there moving toward you, love and rescue in his arms.

Hannah's Lament

In her deep anguish Hannah prayed to the LORD, weeping bitterly. And she made a vow, saying, "LORD Almighty, if you will only look on your servant's misery and remember me, and not forget your servant but give her a son, then I will give him to the LORD for all the days of his life, and no razor will ever be used on his head."

As she kept on praying to the LORD, Eli observed her mouth. Hannah was praying in her heart, and her lips were moving but her voice was not heard. Eli thought she was drunk and said to her, "How long are you going to stay drunk? Put away your wine."

"Not so, my lord," Hannah replied, "I am a woman who is deeply troubled. I have not been drinking wine or beer; I was pouring out my soul to the LORD. Do not take your servant for a wicked woman; I have been praying here out of my great anguish and grief."

Eli answered, "Go in peace, and may the God of Israel grant you what you have asked of him."

She said, "May your servant find favor in your eyes." Then she went her way and ate something, and her face was no longer downcast.

1 SAMUEL 1:10-18

3

begin
with
how

Responses to Pain

I SIT ON THE BACK PORCH watching my two oldest sons play soccer and giggle boisterously in the backyard below. Kevin's out for a jog, and our youngest boy went to bed early after a long session of physical therapy. Like many recent evenings, I am once again not feeling well.

I like to fancy myself as a kind of Wonder Woman. (I mean, *obviously* I'm her doppelgänger and often get confused for her. Happens. All. The. Time.) These days, though, I've shed my tiara and lasso for a set of rusty armor. Tonight I'm the Tin Man. My illness—which at this point remains undiagnosed but appears to be some type of fun autoimmune disease—inches its way, nondescriptly and bilaterally, throughout my body, from top to toe. Though everything hurts, it's my hands that suffer most. My fingers are currently frozen in unpliable, angry fists.

I don't want to miss out on the boys' playtime. I refuse to let this disease rob me of these precious days with them. So I do my best to cheer them on from my back-porch view. I also want to continue answering the invitation of this suffering.

I have my journal outside with me to keep at the work of lament that began at the concert that night. Since most laments are expressed verbally or visually, I sense that whatever this process involves, it will help if I can write down a few things. That is, if I can figure out how to grasp a pen. Tin Man's hands being what they are and all. *How do I even begin responding to pain?* I wonder.

Reacting to Pain

There are a variety of human responses to pain. Some people, when faced with suffering, soar. But for others—maybe even for you—suffering can drive our faith into the ground. It deeply impacts our walk with God, and not always in a positive way. What once was everything—our faith, our devotion to Jesus, our unwavering love for him—can sadly transform into a small, unrecognizable thing, a mound of dirt and earth and mess and doubt and questions and frustrations. We might still pray and sing worship songs and have our "quiet times," but deep inside, we feel like we may as well be talking to the ceiling fan.

In their classic book on discipleship, authors Janet Hagberg and Robert Guelich write that one of the most crucial stages in the life of a Christian is what they coin "The Journey Inward." It's at this stage that our doubts and disappointments grow more and more unmanageable.

> If we have been people of strong faith, our life, though not necessarily easy, has fit nicely into our faith framework. Then the event or crisis often takes on major proportions. It often strikes close to our core, for example, our children, spouse, work, or health. For the first time, our faith does not seem to work. We feel remote, immobilized, unsuccessful, hurt, ashamed, or reprehensible. Neither our faith nor God provides what we need to soothe us, heal us, answer our prayers, fulfill our wishes, change our circumstances, or solve our problems. Our formula of faith, whatever that may have been, does not work any more, or so it appears. We are stumped, hurting, angry, betrayed, abandoned, unheard, or unloved. Many simply want to give up. Their life of faith may even seem to have been a fraud at worst, a mirage at best.[1]

Many people walk away from their faith at this point in their journey. You and I have seen this happen. They (or we) begin to doubt. Soon, doubting leads to desolation. Desolation results in a departure from Christianity altogether.

If we don't walk away from our faith, another possible response to pain is to pretend that it doesn't exist. We suck it up. Compartmentalize. Pretend, as I have done for so long.

But as we all know, denial typically ends up hurting us or our loved ones—because emotions tend to dwell near the surface, just waiting to explode. In other words, we can move all our trash to the attic and try to hide it from ourselves and the neighbors, but sooner or later, the whole house is going to stink.

Or perhaps we attempt to escape the reality of pain. We drink or overeat. (I personally binge-watch British television shows on Netflix.) We shop. We sleep. We stop sleeping. We become addicted people. Soon, we realize that pretending something isn't there only gives it more power.

Kevin and I lived in Zambia for a time, and one of our Zambian friends recently remarked about our American tendency to escape or fake. He had just finished watching the movie *Creed*, the Rocky reboot from 2015, and was laughing about it. "You Americans!" he said. "You just think that a bunch of hard work and 'doing it on your own' will get you through rough times. All of your movies are like that. You just 'rise above.' No one suffers for longer than a half hour."

He's right. None of us want to suffer long. We like to think of affliction as something to rush through, strut successfully away from, and then talk about during an inspirational keynote address at a conference. The problem is that when we're in the heart of our Inward Journey, none of those options—walking away, faking, or escaping—actually leads to true healing.

Lament asks us to do something out of the ordinary. It invites us to sit with our grief, no matter how uncomfortable. In the words of Eugene Peterson, lament says, "When life is heavy and hard to take, go off by yourself. Enter the silence. Bow in prayer. Don't ask questions: Wait for hope to appear."[2]

Lament calls us away from our typical responses to pain and asks us to simply stay put until God does something. But how, practically speaking, do we even do that?

The How of Lament

No matter how you're currently responding to your pain, and no matter how long you've been living with it, the book of Lamentations offers us all some helpful guidance for beginning a lament journey. Generally assumed to be written by Jeremiah, "the weeping prophet,"[3] Lamentations is four individual-yet-united acrostic poems, plus a non-acrostic fifth poem. Each line of the poems begins with a successive letter of the Hebrew alphabet.[4] Some believe this structure was created so that Hebrew children could easily memorize God's Word. Others note that Jeremiah was following the traditional structure of Hebrew poetry. Either way—whether he was teaching children, following a poetic pattern, doing both, or building something entirely different, Jeremiah carefully and deliberately crafted one of the world's most powerful laments.

Jeremiah begins his lament with this profound word: *ekah* (other spellings of the word include *hkya* or *'eka*), the Hebrew word for *how*.[5] In fact, in the Hebrew Scriptures, Lamentations is actually titled Ekah.[6]

How is a blunt declaration. "How deserted lies the city!" laments Jeremiah. "How like a widow is she!"[7]

How is also an unadulterated question, something we'd

demand of a friend or loved one who betrayed us: "How could you! How dare you! How are we supposed to move past this?"

As we learn to lament, we must begin the same way—by following Jeremiah's example. We ask. We demand. We declare our own ekahs.

At times our ekahs are raw: *God, how could you allow this? I hate this. Are you actually as good as I've always believed?*

On other occasions, our ekahs are a simple acknowledgment: *Oh how this stings!* At other times, repentant: *How sorry I am, God. I have betrayed you once more.*

Still, in other moments, our ekahs, like Jeremiah's, are on behalf of others. *God, so many people live with such toxic pain, in such oppressive circumstances. How will you fix this? This is too horrible, God. Look at how your people are suffering. Step in and do something!*

We can throw all of our ekahs at God without fear; he won't punish us for our honest emotions. So stop faking. Quit escaping. Don't walk away from him. In as much power as I have to do so, I give you permission to start now. Yell, scream, cry, paint, draw, pray, sing. Choose an ekah journal and start writing. Whatever you do, just talk to God openly and freely. He can take it. Pour out your sadness and frustration as often as you need to, for as long as you need to.

If you need a starting place, take a look at one of David's most famous songs, Psalm 13, a fearless example of an ekah-filled lament:

How long, LORD? Will you forget me forever?
How long will you hide your face from me?

How long must I wrestle with my thoughts
    and day after day have sorrow in my heart?
How long will my enemy triumph over me?

Look on me and answer, LORD my God.
    Give light to my eyes, or I will sleep in death,
and my enemy will say, "I have overcome him,"
    and my foes will rejoice when I fall.

But I trust in your unfailing love;
    my heart rejoices in your salvation.
I will sing the LORD's praise,
    for he has been good to me.

Like Jeremiah, David doesn't run from his sorrow or pretend that it doesn't exist. He hurls his most vulnerable ekahs at God, over and over again. This isn't a gentle surrendering; it's a reckoning, a list of the absurd ways David has felt abandoned by God. You can hear the desperation, the anguish of David's soul. "Look at me and answer!" he demands. *Don't betray me. Don't forget me. Don't disappoint me. How long? How long? How long?*

Then somehow in the middle of his outburst, David shifts his tone: "But I trust in your unfailing love." David's reaction to pain begins with complaint but eventually and mysteriously moves to praise. David's misery hasn't dissipated. His enemies are still threatening to celebrate his downfall. But still, somehow, David sings his louder song. Somehow David has learned to trust the God who initially appeared untrustworthy.

On the other side of the Inward Journey, "we are on our way to more complete healing, which entails a deeper awareness of our weaknesses. We can hear, see, touch, and smell the God of our salvation. We are becoming intimate with God in the fullest sense of the word *intimate*."[8]

As we learn to surrender our ekahs to God, we are actually letting God loose from the neat and tidy boxes we've placed him in. We are letting God be God. As this new intimacy with God transforms us, our laments are transformed as well.

My Ekahs

As for my own lament journey here on my back porch—watching my boys play soccer while my body flares with pain—all of my ekahs pinball around in my brain, and I struggle to know what to *do* with them, how to actually offer them to God.

I look up at the Chicago evening sky. It's a little hazy because of the city lights, but I can see a few stars punctuating the darkness. I rub my right hand gently, warming it up, preparing it to write. My oldest son notices me and senses that something is wrong. He takes a quick break from the game and shouts at me, "Mom, ya doing okay?" I answer my precious kid, "I don't feel great, buddy. But that's okay. I love you guys. Keep playing."

At last, I stop overthinking it, open up my journal, and simply begin. I start by writing down my ekahs, just to get them out of my head—which is difficult not only emotionally but also physically. Doing this, writing down my ekahs, feels like an act of lament in and of itself. Here are some of my first *hows*:

- *How could you allow Cameron to die in such a horrific manner? The remaining mysteries around it are unbearable. Your Word says, you will "[keep] our feet from slipping."⁹ Is that just a joke?*

- *How could you let me get sick, God? I can barely function, and my kids are so little! How will this impact them in the long run? Do you even see my family here?*

- *How will Kevin and I get through this? We build walls more than support each other. If you don't intervene, I don't know if we'll make it.*

- *How do I keep working? How do I keep going? How can I do what you've built me to do?*

- *How will Nolan's spinal-cord issues and life-threatening allergies affect him in the long term? How will he have a reasonable life? How will he go to school? How will he exist in the world? How could you have let this happen to my boy?*

- *How can I grieve my own pain when there is much greater suffering in the world?*

- *How are you going to show up? What are your plans here? Do something! Step in!*

And the last one, a declaration:

- *How lonely, scared, angry, and sad I feel. You've let me down, God. And I don't know if I'm "supposed" to say that. But that's how I feel. All I know right now is your absence. Look on me and answer.*

I look over my list of ekahs. I would like to yell them at the top of my lungs, honestly. But I don't want to scare the kids. So instead, I imagine scattering each one around God's throne, a messy pile of questions without answers at his feet.

I want him to pick them up, one by one, and tuck them carefully into his breast pocket. I want him to store them like a treasure, safely near his heart. If not that, then I want him to plant them in a garden, little seedlings that grow into something fragrant and lovely, something he watches, waters, and carefully tends to.

———◆———

There's this story about Jesus where he spits on the ground, mixing dirt and saliva together to form a muddy concoction. He rubs the mixture onto the eyes of a blind man, giving him sight. If at the moment your walk with Jesus and your lament journey are nothing more than a mess of dirt, mud, and spit, take courage. That's enough material to see your way to *how*—to stop faking, escaping, or running away and stay put in your grief, while waiting for hope once again to appear.

A Lament by David: A Maskil (A Teaching Lament)

My heart is in anguish within me;
    the terrors of death have fallen on me.
Fear and trembling have beset me;
    horror has overwhelmed me.
I said, "Oh, that I had the wings of a dove!
    I would fly away and be at rest.

I would flee far away
    and stay in the desert;
I would hurry to my place of shelter,
    far from the tempest and storm. . . .
As for me, I call to God,
    and the LORD saves me.
Evening, morning and noon
    I cry out in distress,
    and he hears my voice.
He rescues me unharmed
    from the battle waged against me. . . .
Cast your cares on the LORD
    and he will sustain you;
he will never let
    the righteous be shaken.

PSALM 55:4-8, 16-18, 22

4

the
grief
of
love

Lamenting
Losses

WHEN MY KIDS CATCH A glimpse of lightning bugs for the first time one summer, they assume they're battery powered. "Are those little flashlights attached to anything?" they ask.

"Those aren't flashlights," I reply. "That's God's little magic trick. Wanna know something else?" I continue. "Those lightning bugs got me through one of the worst summers of my childhood."

They're awestruck when I tell them about the summer I cut my foot open with glass. I show them the faded checkmark scar that's still on the underside of my foot. "I wasn't allowed to ride my bike or climb trees that summer. So I spent most evenings catching fireflies in mason jars."

They grab jars from the kitchen and try to catch their own magic lightning in a bottle. I watch them and find myself feeling nostalgic for the invincibility of childhood. If we step on broken glass, we won't cut our feet. If we jump, our mom or dad will catch us. If we want to find magic, we need only look for a firefly.

As we mature, of course, we learn to accept the frustration of our own limitedness and the limitations of others. We learn that actions do have consequences, that the firefly's glow is nothing more than a chemical reaction called bioluminescence. We learn that the world is more complicated than we ever could have imagined.

Yet when we watch little children run around the backyard, spotting fireflies for the first time, we remember, don't we—that even in life's complication, childhood wonder and abundance still exist. It just takes a bit of love to help draw it out of us again.

"Come on, Mom. Help us," they beg. So I chase the boys around the backyard, playing tickle monster, all of us a bundle of giggles and glee.

When Cameron goes missing, it's my inner child—the one who still believes in the magic of lightning bugs—that hurts the most.

Permanent Laments

It is a few months after that firefly night when the call comes. Kevin, the boys, and I are playing a round of cards. We're trash-talking and laughing, enjoying some more silly family time together, when my phone interrupts our fun. My mother is on the other end, saying something I can't quite make sense of. Something about how Cameron was hiking in Oregon. "Please pray." I catch that and the next few words. "Please help us call the Oregon Park Service." Three years later, the Crater Lake park ranger's number is still EXPO'd on the whiteboard in my kitchen.

Putting together clues and tracks, the best guess we can come up with is that Cameron, my cousin and childhood friend, fell from a snow-covered cornice into the startlingly beautiful blue waters of Crater Lake—a two-thousand-foot-deep body of water described by most as the closest thing to heaven on earth.

The night of Cam's funeral, his rugby buddies and our family drink Irish whiskey and sing country-music songs and release paper lanterns into the night.[1] We stand there for a very long time, watching the lanterns float across the starry Nashville sky. Some lanterns unite and form the letter C, as if they are honoring Cameron with us. Even now, in the daylight, my aunt, Cameron's mom, notices clouds in the shape of the letter C. She can't help but wonder if it's her imagination or a supernatural gift of love. "Hugs from heaven," she calls them. I desperately want the cloud-Cs to be a good gift from God. But as I wade through my ekahs, this one in particular is the most difficult to process. *How could you not protect him, God? Where were you?*

Like most of us do in grief, I want to make sense of nonsense. I want my ekahs answered so that I can write a good sermon on the topic. But there are no remains of Cameron and also oh-so-many remains: the gorgeous photo of Crater Lake he texted before his fall, all of our lingering questions, all of our memories and stories.

[Where is the hope in a tragic, sudden death like his? Where is God's presence in freak accidents? How do you find God's love in a thing that feels so loveless?)

God, can your love show up, even here? My sister-in-law, who knows me well, texts me encouraging words every now and then. Usually along the lines of "You don't have to have all the answers, Aubrey. It's okay to just be sad."

"To the 'why' of suffering we get no firm answer,"[2] writes Nicholas Wolterstorff, as he laments his own son (who died in a fashion eerily similar to Cameron). Some suffering is the result of sin and the world's brokenness. Other suffering is the result of corrupt leadership. Some suffering we bring on ourselves. But not all suffering is the *clear result* of something. Not all suffering is reasonable. Not all agonizing questions can be answered sensibly, especially in losses like these. In our deepest grief, we don't lament to find answers. We lament to stop searching for them. We lament to be still in the unanswerable.

But without answers, how can I explain this type of loss to my kids? "Uncle" Cam, who just carried you in his arms, who just showed you the inside of his plane, who just sent you postcards from Rome, is now no longer with us. How can I tell three precious, expectant, and innocent faces that we simply have to learn to live with grief? We have to keep going. We do life. We still have to empty the dishwasher and fold the laundry and do our homework and feed the fish. The only difference is that we are changed as we do it. An altered person sets the table today.

My aunt experiences her laments the only way a mom can—in her bones, in her body. After all, laments are not just cognitive exercises; lament demands to be felt.[3] She knew physical pain at his birth and here she is, laboring again—pushing, groaning through unbearable pain.

Because she is so uniquely impacted by Cameron's death, I know it's probably unfair of me to look to her to learn how to grieve. Still, I find that she is helping me find God's love in this. She and my uncle have such huge hearts. They start a scholarship in Cameron's name. They build a memorial bench at Crater Lake. They bless others. They scatter love everywhere they go.

When I ask her how she is processing things, sometimes she cries. Other times, she quotes Charles Spurgeon: "God is too good to be unkind and too wise to be mistaken. When we cannot trace his hand, we must trust his heart."[4]

She tells me that she is trying—"Lord knows, I try." But she doesn't always understand. "Some days are better than others. I keep praying for good days. I keep asking *how*, *why*, and *why now*, but those answers don't come."

There are many evenings when I continue to ask my ekahs and receive no answer. I yell and scream at God for doing this to our family. I refuse to walk with him. I tell him I don't believe in him anymore.

Of course, the irony is that the whole time, I'm still talking to God. And he lets me.

As David laments his beloved Jonathan, he doesn't ask why. He simply declares this well-known ekah, "How the mighty have fallen. . . . I grieve for you, Jonathan my brother; you were very dear to me."[5]

It's easy to blame God for my grief. But in time, I realize that I am not grieving for anything God did or didn't do.

I am grieving for you, Cameron, my brother. You were very dear to me. Empty chairs sit at empty tables that once were full of you.[6]

Lightning Bugs

Years after Cameron's death, his body remains undiscovered. But we soon discover something else. Our world changes around us once again.

A woman comes forward with two young sons and proof of paternity. If this offends your sensibilities, then perhaps you should skip ahead a few paragraphs, because I refuse to apologize for two precious boys who have Cameron's blue eyes, goofy grin, and light blond hair. I won't say sorry, for their mom, a giving soul who loved Cam, assures us that her relationship with him was exactly what she wanted, and promises us that he never abandoned her or the boys.

She generously shares her sons—children we never knew existed—with our entire family. She invites us to know them, to love them, to buy them Christmas presents.

It's a complicated situation, certainly, filled with questions of integrity, concerns, confusion, and what-ifs. Of course we wonder, *What in the world was Cameron doing, thinking? What was this secret life he was living?* Yet we can't deny that this is still very much a gift. My aunt and uncle have become grandparents once more—a dream they thought was forever washed away in the waters of Crater Lake. My sons have new cousins. We all have a return for our loss. We have loved within our grief, and our grief has returned us love.

God never swept in like Superman to fix this, never traveled back in time to stop it from happening. God never truly answered my grief-ekahs the way I wanted him to.

Instead, he did something else, something wild and bewildering. He "Already'd" in our Not Yet. If grief has been my Shalom lament, then God has answered this *not good* with his *very good*. The love I was longing for, asking for, here it is. Right in the middle of my most painful lament, stand two tangible, touchable, and tactile boys—two magic lightning bugs in the darkness—in the shape of God's love.

Sometimes, it's only in looking back that we see clearly. As I look back now, even in this horrible circumstance, I can see God's hand of love touching everything.

God's love is in the encouraging texts from my sister-in-law. God's love is in the kindness of the park ranger allowing a memorial bench to take up space on national park property. God's love is in the tearful phone calls with my aunt, in the photo Cam sent us before he died. God's love was even with Cameron as he died, doing what he most enjoyed. God's love is in the symbols, symbols that we were created to need—the Cs in the sky, the floating lanterns, the tattoos we all eventually got in Cam's honor, and a million more like them. God's love has shown up in all of these miniature miracles and, of course, in the giant miracles of these two boys. Instead of answering our ekahs, God shows up in them.

Surely this is a God who restores our fortunes. Surely

this is a God who transforms our good-byes into hellos. Surely this is a God in whom all lament songs become love songs.

This is why, even in my darkest days of doubting God and in my heaviest grief, I have continued to go to the Communion table each Sunday morning. In Jesus' body broken, in his blood shed, in his suffering, he embodied love for us. Week by week, I need the reminder that suffering is not something to pass the time, not a test we have to pass. It is the *"means of which,"* writes N. T. Wright, "the rescuing love of God is poured out into the world."[7]

Love

"Have you ever felt unloved?" I ask my boys one morning at breakfast.

My middle son, who bubbles with joy and confidence on the outside but has a swirling inner emotional life, responds. He allows himself to be vulnerable. He knuckles away tears as he tells us that sometimes the kids at school say they are "unfriending" him. It makes him mad. It hurts his feelings. He feels unloved.

This moment feels holy, my son opening up about his pain. So I tread lightly; I don't want it to pass because I became overbearing. I stay quiet, and in a moment of unexpected brotherly kindness, I hear my other sons speak into his hurt. "Come find us at recess," they tell him. "We won't unfriend you."

I bask in this display of love between my sons and finally add my two cents. "I am so sorry, honey," I say. "I wish that wasn't happening. That would make me sad and mad too. Sometimes there are bad things in life, and they can really hurt us. Sometimes friends are mean, or we get sick, or sad things happen.

"I have sometimes been very upset at God for Cameron's death. But I want you to know this: No matter how hard and sad things get, no matter how angry we get, God's love reaches down through the hurt and marks us. It changes us. It transforms us. In the midst of darkness, we can find unexpected surprises like brothers who won't unfriend us, no matter how sad we get."

It's above their heads, I know. But I hope one day they will understand—just as I hope you will also understand—that though suffering and tragedy are not the exceptions in this life, love is the extraordinary surprise that accompanies our grief.

Death feels like the opposite of love. And yet God showed us his own love in dying for us, in overcoming death for us. So are death and love opposites after all? In Jesus, perhaps not. In him, one can be the means to the other.

A Lament Song by the Sons of Korah

LORD, you are the God who saves me;
   day and night I cry out to you.
May my prayer come before you;
   turn your ear to my cry.

I am overwhelmed with troubles
   and my life draws near to death.

I am counted among those who go down to the pit;
    I am like one without strength. . . .

You have put me in the lowest pit,
    in the darkest depths. . . .

Are your wonders known in the place of darkness,
    or your righteous deeds in the land of oblivion?

But I cry to you for help, LORD;
    in the morning my prayer comes before you.
Why, LORD, do you reject me
    and hide your face from me?

From my youth I have suffered and been close
       to death;
   I have borne your terrors and am in despair.
Your wrath has swept over me;
    your terrors have destroyed me.
All day long they surround me like a flood;
    they have completely engulfed me.
You have taken from me friend and neighbor—
    darkness is my closest friend.

PSALM 88:1-4, 6, 12-18

yet

Pam's Lament

ONE OF THE LAMENT CRIES of my heart was born from a sense of loneliness. I didn't think anyone would ever understand the physical, emotional, and psychological toll of chronic illness. But God is faithful and sets the lonely in families (Psalm 68:6). In fact, sometimes God puts the chronically ill in families with other chronically ill people.

My mother-in-law, Pam, has lived with an autoimmune disease for over forty years. As she's been through major surgeries, medication changes, and emotional ups and downs, she has been a torchlight for so many, including me. She listens, guides, leads, and understands. Most importantly, she always brings me—and others—back to Jesus. If you find yourself in pain today, may Pam's example strengthen you.

Pam

I'm sharing my story, not because it is great, but because God is.

I always had a plan for everything. My family, friends, and coworkers knew this, and it was apparent to most around me that I was always formulating some way to orchestrate an objective. I still find a good amount of comfort in stating the obvious. Family meals and events are not an exception: "You get your plate here, food here, utensils and drinks here, and then sit down and eat." I was, and still am, tolerated with love for my need to order things.

I love creativity, but I also love discipline and diligence. That's how I planned to live as a wife, mom, businesswoman, volunteer, and tennis player. I kept my life and my household afloat with calendars, chore lists, and well-executed plans.

Then came my diagnosis—and along with it, a lot of drugs and dietary changes and a lot of people with good ideas about how to address it. I just knew that whatever I did, I wanted to do it aggressively. I wanted a plan.

Everyone who has faced illness has a unique story and journey. The difficulty is that there is not a lot of predictability. Sometimes there isn't a cure. Other times, there isn't closure. After a number of tests and surgeries, it was clear that my disease was invading my entire body and my well-made plans for life.

In August of 2013, I was physically and emotionally exhausted from years of trying to be in control of my plans, from medicines and surgeries and diets. I stood at the back door of our cute little Cape Cod rental home and said aloud, "God, it is all yours. It always has been. Forgive me for my faithlessness, for trying to control. It is all on you and it is about you."

It was unquestionably a holy moment when I knew and felt his presence.

The next day, I woke up and couldn't move my arms or legs, couldn't open my eyes, had difficulty hearing. I could talk because I remember asking if my family was there. They were. I remember humming old hymns. I remember asking if someone would read Scripture aloud to me. Mine was a quiet mind and a stilled body, but Jesus was alive there with me. There were a lot of doctors, tests, drugs, and differing diagnoses, depending on the medical specialty. It did not make a lot of sense and, quite honestly, it still doesn't. I remember very clearly knowing that I was resting in God's sovereign plan, whatever it was. My intense need for understanding and answers was replaced by God himself. Chronic pain can be an evil taskmaster—yet, when surrendered to God, it can be a reminder of our human frailty and God's awesome love and redemption.

Today, I am mostly recovered, but the medical details of those days remain a mystery, and the disease continues. Every morning when I wake up now, I don't go through "my plan" for the day with the Lord. Instead, my heart says, "Lord, this day is on you. It is yours, Jesus. I surrender it all to you to accomplish whatever you will. Please let it be full of holy moments with you."

5
hitting
walls
in
lament

When You'd Rather
Not Face Your Pain

"MA'AM, YOU ABSOLUTELY cannot carry a snow globe onto
the airplane. It contains too much liquid content. Unless you
want to break it open and drink it, it's not going anywhere
with you."

I'd like to break you *open.* (I think this but don't actually
say it aloud because I'd rather not be arrested at the airport
in front of my children.) Sometimes suffering is supposed to
transform you, "make you nourishment for other people," as
Oswald Chambers wrote.[1] Sometimes pain just makes you
angry.

"What do you mean I can't take the snow globe on the

plane? This is a gift. For a family member. A young girl who is *in mourning*."

Kevin, the boys, and I are traveling from Chicago to Colorado for the holidays, to Cameron's favorite mountain, so that we can remember him together, in his favorite place. It's two months into my battle with my still-undiagnosed illness, and I've started a new medication regime. In case my TSA meltdown-in-progress isn't enough of a clue, them are some crazy pills.

The Snow Globe Embargo would have been enough to set me off. But my confused emotions about my illness, mixed with my grief over Cameron, sprinkled with the aforementioned crazy pills, create a cocktail of . . . how shall I put this? I think the technical term I'm searching for is *rage*. Yes. I'm a rager. So I do what anyone in my shoes would: I snatch the snow globe from the TSA officer and try to make my escape.

Unfortunately, I'm not the nimblest of humans.

"Ma'am, you need to remove your hands from the snow globe or we will have to escort you back through security." At this point, another TSA officer arrives on the scene, just to prove the point. My poor husband is off to the side, burying his head in his phone, Googling what I can only assume is, "What to do when your wife is thrown in jail." My kids are scanning the airport crowd for another mommy. *We don't belong to that scary lady over there.*

I release the snow globe but reach into my purse for my phone to take a photo of it. Looking back on the incident—with the nature of heightened security in airports being what it is these days—this is perhaps a mistake. Both officers grab me by the arms. "Ma'am, take your hand out of your purse immediately. What do you think you're doing?"

"I'm just getting my phone, okay? *Calm down.* All I want to do is take a picture of the snow globe. If you won't let me travel with it, I at least want a photo of it. Like I said before, it's for a little girl. A little girl in mourning. A little girl in mourning *at Christmas!*"

"Ma'am, you need to put your cell phone away. This snow globe is now property of TSA. You cannot take a picture of it."

"What do you mean I can't take a picture of the snow globe?" And if you thought I spiraled before, just wait. I actually yell, "THIS IS MY SNOW GLOBE!" (By the way, no one in the history of verbal communication ever uttered the words *snow globe* so many times in one exchange.)

"We will give you one final warning," the first TSA officer declares. "If you can't calm down, you will not be able to travel today."

At this point, I throw my hands up in the air, gesticulate dramatically, and announce with ferocious holiday cheer, "Well, merry freaking Christmas, TSA!"

The second TSA officer responds, "Ma'am, please don't get mad at us for doing our job."

Since I previously showed restraint, having not said the earlier thing about breaking the first TSA officer open, I decide it is perfectly acceptable to say this: "Well, your job sucks!" (I mean, the guy was basically asking for it.)*

I make a run for it. I sprint away from TSA as fast as my

---

* I would like to state for the record that I am a huge fan of TSA. Thank you for keeping our airways safe. Sorry for being a brat. It wasn't you; it was my meds. Except I do have to mention that last winter, you somehow lost *one* of my favorite boots as it went through the security checkpoint, forcing me to walk around O'Hare in one shoe. They were really cute boots, just so you know. The one really misses the other.

(hurting) legs will carry me. Dashing past Kevin and the kids, I yell at them to meet me at the moving sidewalk. Once they find me, Kev begins to slow clap. "Great job, Aubs. Real good example for our children there."

Then come the tears. Crying on the moving sidewalk. Crying at the airport Starbucks. Crying on the tarmac. Crying as we prepare for takeoff. Crying as the flight attendants tell us to provide ourselves with oxygen masks before we hand them to our respective children. Crying, not because of the crazy pills, but because of my embarrassment, anger, and shame. Well, probably a little bit because of the crazy pills.

As it turns out, sometimes I hit a wall in all this lamenting. Sometimes, lament looks a lot less like acceptance and a lot more like frenzy.

I'm supposed to be embarking on this meaningful lament journey—expressing my ekahs, finding glimpses of God's love in my grief, moving through an Exodus journey, being transformed by suffering, all the while gathering all manner of profound wisdom and meaningful life lessons, et cetera. But here I am on this airplane, sobbing over that stupid snow globe, and I feel stuck and embarrassed—unable to lament well and actually not wanting to lament at all. I don't want to bring this to God. I don't want to surrender my ekahs to him. I don't care anymore. I just want to feel sorry for myself awhile.

In Jeffery Eugenides' intricate novel *The Marriage Plot*, the protagonist, at a low point in his struggle with illness, asks an acute question: "'Where's Leonard?' he kept asking. . . . Where was the guy who could write a twenty-page paper on

Spinoza with his left hand while playing chess with his right?
... 'Where's Leonard?' Leonard asked. Leonard didn't know."[2]

If you're in a painful season yourself, you may understand Leonard's dilemma. Equipped with my new disease, I often wonder that very thing. *Where's Aubrey?* This woman crying on the airplane is certainly not the woman I know myself to be. My brain and body, once sturdy vessels of satisfaction and action, now regularly melt into puddles of pain and inertia. I have become dysfunctional and unreliable, unpredictable.

Do you want to know the real truth, though? I'm not only questioning who I've become; I am asking the question that all have asked in times of suffering, the oldest cliché question in the book, really. If God truly loves me—and if he is actually a good God—why would he allow this to happen?

Feel free to call me a big baby, but I don't want to be sitting on an airplane thinking about my sick self, while also trying to deduce where the real me has gone, all while grieving the loss of Cameron and wondering where God is in the midst of everything. I don't want to do the hard work of being still in suffering today. I just want to blast into the future when all will be well again, when I'll feel like myself again.

I want to move quickly from my ekahs, my *How could yous*, to the transformation. I want to slap on a Band-Aid and move on. I want to skip the yucky part. I want to skip lament.

But (sigh) I won't.

I reach into the carry-on bag at my feet, pull out my journal, and write a new ekah: "How do I do this when I just really don't want to?"

The *Supposed To*s of Suffering

If you are in a suffering season, or walking with someone who is, you know there are a lot of *supposed to*s. We're *supposed to* be able to step back from our negative experiences, shake them up like a snow globe, and see what settles—what's the big life lesson we're meant to learn?

We're *supposed to* be some great example of strength. Suffering is *supposed to* bring wisdom and perspective. Pain is *supposed to* give you the ability to sort the important from the superfluous—what stays? What goes? What's worth focusing on when your focus becomes limited? Suffering is even *supposed to* make you more compassionate toward others. And the reality is, I believe those *supposed to*s are true. As my dear friend Tara, who lost her best friend in a car accident, once texted me, "Sorrow makes us better people. Not that the pain is any less crappy, but it can, somehow, actually change us for the better."

If I'm honest (and I'm going to be), my first instinct in this book was to lean into the *supposed to*s. I had a whole list of lies that sounded really good. Stuff like *pain is teaching me how to be present* and *pain is teaching me perspective* and *pain is teaching me to craft.* (I got briefly and intensely crafty while on loads and loads of steroids and made precisely one wreath. It will hang in my bathroom forever.)

If you're anything like me on the airplane, you might not want to become an object lesson anyway. I'm certainly not in the mood to learn some great moral of the story. I just want the pain and the sadness to be shaken up and disappear to the bottom. I want to cling to my rage. I like it. It's my little pet. In fact, I want other people to be afraid of my rage and, because of it, give me special permission to smuggle illegal snow globes across the country.

I want to stop asking questions about who God is in the midst of me not recognizing who I am anymore. I want to give up. This is too hard.

Who Am I? Who Is God?

In Jerusalem's anti-Cinderella story, we find out early on the reason for her fall from grace. Lamentations 1 tells us of Jerusalem's "many sins" (verse 5), including allowing pagan nations to enter her sanctuary, something God had expressly forbidden.

To give you an idea of just how horrifying things were for Jeremiah and the Israelites, the siege of Jerusalem lasted about two years. By month four, the Israelites had zero access to food. When the Babylonian soldiers finally broke through Jerusalem's protective city wall, they violated and ravished her women (Lamentations 5:11), slaughtered her soldiers and rulers, and set fire to the Lord's Temple. Many Israelites were forced to flee their homes. For those who remained, things became awful. The hunger became so unbearable, Jeremiah infers that the Israelite people turned to cannibalism (Lamentations 2:20 and 4:10). You can read more about the brutal siege in 2 Kings 25. It's easy to understand why Jeremiah wondered if death would be better than this suffering (Lamentations 4:9).

Beyond the living nightmare, there existed an overarching question of Israel's identity as God's people.[3] If God was willing to allow his children to endure such horror, were they actually God's beloved to begin with? Was God as loving and compassionate as he had declared himself to be? As German theologian Claus Westermann wrote, "How can God bring such profound suffering upon his people—if they are indeed his people—when he has previously done such great things for them?"[4]

But consider this: The fall of Jerusalem was God's response to the Israelites' disobedience and idolatry. As horrifying as it was, there was a reason for it.

How much more difficult are these questions of God and of our relationship to God, when the suffering we endure isn't a consequence of disobedience? How much harder is it to cry out to God when we can't find any explanation for it?

While I never want to oversimplify or minimize the atrocities endured by Judah, I do want you to know this—even in their sin and idolatry, even in the middle of this terrible siege, even in the midst of their identity crisis, God was there—faithful to his covenant love, never truly abandoning them.

In the same way, God is with you now, drawing you near, providing for your needs, never letting you go, even if you can't find rhyme or reason in what's happening to you. In the midst of all the overpowering and conflicting emotions you might be feeling—including the desire to give up and walk away—you can cling to one thing: God's response does not depend on you. God's response to your suffering depends on God, and God hasn't changed in the midst of your pain.

As Westermann noted, "God does not punish those who remonstrate or rise up against him; rather, he gives sustenance to those who hunger and water to those who thirst. . . . The lament of those who suffer is heard by God—even though in desperation their lament is turned against God, even though it is an accusation against God. Even he who despairs is within range of God's ear!"[5])

What that means is, at the end of the day, it doesn't really matter if you hit a wall in lament. It doesn't really matter if you can't get enough clarity to react in a super positive way to the experience. It doesn't really matter if your lament is perfect or orderly. It doesn't really matter if you embarrass yourself in front of your family, some TSA agents, and the entire city of Chicago. You get to feel what you feel and don't have to try to force yourself to transcend the moment as you lament. In fact, you don't have to do much; just let him love you—you and all of your mixed emotions, too. God's love will transform you. You don't have to force it.

Spring in Winter

Kevin, the boys, and I arrive in Colorado without any further snow-globe ado. I fear, initially, that the cold air will damage my already aching joints, put my foul mood into a worse one. Surprisingly, though, winter is a nurse. She lifts me out of my pain, comforts and rocks me, and reminds me to be playful again.

Kevin and the boys and I sled, ice-skate, build snowmen, and drive around town, looking at Christmas lights. Just like the night of his funeral, we once again light our floating lanterns for Cameron. It's become our lament tradition. We tell stories of his smile and cry communal tears. My aunt and uncle talk of finding God in their deepest grief, in inexplicable and miraculous moments. We drink hot chocolate and hot toddies and eat fresh, warm cinnamon rolls. Kevin and I start to thaw and become blankets for each other instead of ramparts against. It's not everything, but it's enough to be a foreshadowing. We have more struggles to come, but there's hope for us yet.

In the crisp Colorado air, God reveals glimpses of a singing, blossoming spring. God has waited patiently with me in the midst of all my anger and questions, faithful and unchanging. He waits until I'm able to surface for air, waits to help me see glimpses of goodness. Lament in this season hasn't meant forcing the lesson. Lament in the midst of my anger has meant being honest with God and myself about this shaky ground I'm on, until I realize the steadiness of the one who's holding me.

Although I will forever carry this illness—and the empty space where Cameron used to fit—this trip feels important somehow, like it might be my first taste of healing. I know it shouldn't take a vacation to hear God's voice, but it's here in the winter air where I finally sense some warmth. It's here where I finally realize that my identity hasn't shifted and neither has God's. On the plane ride home, in fact, God brings to mind a reminder of his steadfastness.

Before I was sick, I used to run a lot, several miles a day. But I wasn't always a good runner. I was slow and clumsy and insecure about my running abilities. The first time Kevin and I were out jogging together, I kept apologizing to him. "I'm not fast enough. I'm not a runner. I'm sorry," I kept saying. "Don't stay with me. Just go ahead. It's fine. I'm sorry."

He stopped mid-stride and looked straight at me. "Aubrey, stop apologizing. You're out running. Right now. That makes you a runner. Period."

It was so simple to him—and so healing to me. (Aren't

the most profound things often the most simple?) Kevin gave me permission to keep going, to run at my own pace, and he always stayed with me. We've since run in health and now in sickness, and also like crazy people through airports. He has never left my side, a beautiful image of the unchanging nature of God.

Once, I was a runner. Not because I was ever elegant or fast, but simply because I was running. Just as now, I am the beloved. Not because I handle these hard things with grace and patience, but because I am intimately loved by God.

I imagine you're a more refined person than I am. You probably don't cause a lot of scenes in public. But I can also bet that deep down inside, you have days when you want to tell pain and grief to shove off (and that's being polite). You'd rather not lament at the moment, thank you very much.

If I could burn one thing onto your hurting heart, it would be this: Even though you suffer from this awful thing—no matter how truly terrible it may be—and even though you may not be able to surface for air right now, God has not changed. Who you are to him has not changed. He is utterly faithful, and you are utterly loved. Not because you are healthy or strong or happy, or because you never get angry, or because you handle this thing you face with grace. But simply and profoundly because you are the object of God's fixed delight and affection. Even when you hit walls, even at your messiest, you are his beautiful one.

"See! The winter is past; the rains are over and gone. Flowers appear on the earth; the season of singing has come. . . . Arise, come, my darling," he is saying to you. "My beautiful one, come with me."[6]

A Psalm of Asaph: A Maskil (A Teaching Lament)

O God, why have you rejected us forever?
   Why does your anger smolder against
      the sheep of your pasture?
Remember the nation you purchased long ago,
   the people of your inheritance, whom you
      redeemed—
Mount Zion, where you dwelt.
Turn your steps toward these everlasting ruins,
   all this destruction the enemy has brought
      on the sanctuary . . .

But God is my King from long ago;
   he brings salvation on the earth.

It was you who split open the sea by your power;
   you broke the heads of the monster in the waters . . .
It was you who opened up springs and streams;
   you dried up the ever-flowing rivers.
The day is yours, and yours also the night;
   you established the sun and moon.
It was you who set all the boundaries of the earth;
   you made both summer and winter.

PSALM 74:1-3, 12-13, 15-17

6

we
carry
each other
home

"I JUST DON'T UNDERSTAND why you can't clean the garage,"
Kevin declares one afternoon. He's in a mood. We both are.

I'm experiencing a bad "flare-up." That's what we call it
in the autoimmune disease community when our bodies
attack us. Mine is losing the battle right now, yet the meds
I currently take are pretty little liars. Like the serpent in the
Garden, this medication makes me believe I can do anything
without consequence.

I do things I normally don't. I strip and stain old furni-
ture. I stay up until the wee hours of the morning, paint-
ing and repainting my dining-room walls. I redecorate our

laundry room, of all places. It was a little too cutesy for itself, with a laundry-line-themed wallpaper border: shirts, pants, a denim dress, all billowing in the laundry-line breeze.

I don't actually remove the cutesy border. I just paint over it. I mask it enough to make it seem like an improvement. If the paint peels in the slightest, or if you look close enough, you'll notice the ugly underneath.

But in the midst of this surge of energy, I'm weary from one of suffering's major side effects—relational conflict. My marriage is currently in a flare-up. Mostly, Kevin and I treat each other well. We're polite to each other. But when the clock strikes midnight and the mask slips off, we're all cinder. There's no Ella here.

I fear I've become something my husband doesn't want. He can't possibly be married to a sick wife. I think he needs me to the clean the garage to prove that I am that bouncy bride he married almost twenty years ago. A clean garage is evidence that this isn't actually happening.

Kevin and I try not to let our new reality become us. We attempt to hold it apart and examine it carefully. We make efforts to get mad at the suffering, not at each other. But we can't seem to separate from it, especially the illness part, because this part happens not just *to* me, but *inside* of me. I'm not the wife I once was. I don't have energy to stay up past 8:00 p.m. to hang with Kevin. Every time we try to sit down for a date night, we end up talking about my health and about how we need to adjust as a family because of it. Then we typically end our dates by slamming doors. We let the sun go down on our anger. Our emotions are skyscrapers, high and looming. Our grief is a sunburn, blazing hot. Our pain is a zombie, refusing to stay buried.

We love each other deeply. We're best friends. We are committed to each other before God, for the long haul. But if our marriage is a letter, we are no longer an H, holding hands as equals. We're not an A, leaning on one another. We're not even a T, one carrying the other. If anything, we're a V. Each of us is going in different directions. Both of us trying to escape where we now find ourselves.

Happy Accidents

A few years ago, Kevin decides to run the Chicago Half Marathon. The boys and I make signs, load up in the car, and drive into the city to cheer Dad on. When we arrive downtown, I realize pretty quickly that this is a fool's errand. I can't find a parking spot anywhere.

The boys and I drive around the city of Chicago for over an hour—and that's *after* the hour it takes to get into the city.

On top of the stressful traffic, the app that supposedly keeps track of runners' whereabouts isn't working. I have no clue where Kevin is in the race. He could be finished, for all I know. The boys are getting antsy, afraid we'll miss seeing Daddy run. I am growing more and more road-ragey as every minute passes. "If we can't find a parking place in the next ten minutes," I announce to the boys, "we are going home."

Predictably, they start bawling. "We can't go home," they cry. "We want to see Daddy!"

I take a deep breath and ask the boys to pray with me for a parking spot. To be honest with you, I'm a super-cynical person when it comes to parking-spot prayers. They feel like such a first-world problem. However, the moment we say "Amen," we find a spot. And not just any spot.

We climb out of the car, signs in tow, and walk toward Lake Shore Drive. I'm still unsure if we'll see Kevin, but I figure the boys will enjoy watching the runners. I look down at my phone and push buttons, trying to force the race app to work.

Suddenly, Lincoln starts jumping up and down. "Mom!" he shouts. "There's Dad!"

I respond to him with my parking-spot cynicism. "Honey, that's not Dad. I know you think it's Dad. It may even look like Dad. But there are almost twenty thousand racers here today. This is a thirteen-point-one-mile race. It's not Dad."

"Mom! I mean it! It's Dad! It's Dad!"

I start to argue with him again. But my oldest, the sensible firstborn, stops me. "Mom," he says flatly, "would you just look up? It's Dad."

I look up. It's Dad.

We cheer him on. He waves and smiles. We hold our signs high in the air. I tear up a little. This is a great moment, a meaningful memory for us as a family.

I'm not a statistician. So I don't know the odds of finding the *perfect* parking spot, in the *precise* location, in the *exact* moment my husband will run past us in a thirteen-point-one-mile race made up of almost twenty thousand runners. But I think, *Okay, well, either all of life is random and that was one happy accident, or God is on the throne tending to the little things we care about.*

Now, as the ground shifts beneath us in our marriage, I beg God once more: *Please help us find each other again.*

We need to grieve the loss of something significant in our relationship, but we're avoiding our shared lament.

My marriage ekahs are some of the most delicate. More than *how*s, they are *where*s and *what*s and *when*s and *why*s. *Where are you, O God? What will it take to fix this, O God? When will this end, O God? Why is this so painful, O God?* I spend a lot of days pulling over on sides of roads to cry privately, to scream without being heard.

I don't know how your pain is impacting your relationships. But these trials that should bring us closer to the people we love—a family united against a common enemy—don't always work that way. Sometimes, they do just the opposite.

Imprecatory Laments

In the fourth chapter of Lamentations, Jeremiah speaks to another nation and says something a bit surprising: "Rejoice and be glad, Daughter Edom [the archetypal enemy of Israel[1]]. . . . To you also the cup will be passed; you will be drunk and stripped naked" (Lamentations 4:21).

Them's fightin' words.

In other words, "You're about to get what you deserve. So don't get cocky as you watch us suffer, because you're going to drink the cup of God's wrath too."

In other places in Lamentations, Jeremiah frequently begs God to curse Israel's enemies: "Pay them back what they deserve, LORD. . . . May your curse be on them!" (Lamentations 3:64-65).

These vengeful words are known as imprecatory laments. *Imprecatory* comes from a Latin word literally meaning "the evoking of evil" or "a calling down of evil."² This type of lament is a bitter cry for others to taste the pain we experience. It's a good old-fashioned curse on one's enemies, like Mercutio's famous last words in *Romeo and Juliet*: "A plague o' both your houses!"³

Imprecatory laments are found all throughout the Old Testament. David alone has quite a few imprecatory psalms, which is not totally surprising, considering David's volatile emotional life. In Psalm 58, he cries out ruthlessly, "Break the teeth in their mouths, O God" (verse 6).

But why are imprecatory curses considered laments?

Anger is a natural and common response to painful circumstances. And as I've said before, true lamenting calls for our basest, rawest emotions—even the ugly ones. But anger is usually a secondary emotion, often masking feelings of loneliness, insecurity, shame, abandonment, or sadness.⁴

Anger, all too often, is what chips away at our relationships. The people we love most, the ones we look to for comfort and help, should understand this more than anyone, we reason. But they don't. Our pain is so very individual. Our struggles can feel isolating. We lose each other in the midst of the chaos. And the anger begins. That's why part of the lamenting process is figuring out what the heck is really going on underneath our anger. We need to name our imprecations, to call out the relational infections that are festering under the surface. Only then can we begin to heal our relational wounds.

Ultimately, when we find ourselves cursing our enemies (or even our loved ones), we have to stop and examine ourselves. We need to ask some evaluating questions: *Am I tearing this person down because I'm not getting what I want? Or am I actually witnessing something that God himself hates? Is this godly anger at the injustice and sin in the world? Or do I harbor ungodly hate for this person or people group? What part have I played in this conflict? What's my role? Where do I need to ask God—or this person that I'm imprecating—for forgiveness?*

Anytime you're tempted to imprecate your brother or sister, friend or neighbor, or loved one, try to pause and discern what might really be going on. What's underneath your anger? What might God be showing you in it?

I have imprecated my own husband during this suffering season. I may not be as blatantly vengeful as David or Jeremiah. I certainly don't want Kevin's teeth to fall out. (It would ruin his cute smile.) But this has been my attitude toward him: *I don't really care about how this impacts you. I just want you to experience the same pain I do.* Frankly, we both want the other to drink the cup of suffering we are each privately nursing. Our imprecatory laments toward each other remain silent, but still, so loud.

Home

Okay—I've waited until now to share more about our youngest son's medical struggles, for two reasons. The first is that it's a pretty emotional thing for a mama's heart to relive. The second is because I want to honor his privacy.

But his story connects to my marriage lament in significant ways, so I need to let you in on at least a few pieces of it. The following is what I've been given permission by little Nolan, and by my own mama-heart, to share with you.

Years before this current painful season, ours is a game-changing third pregnancy. We cuddle our youngest son and name him Nolan, meaning "champion," but have no idea that he will be forced to live up to his heroic name.

During his earliest days, our home becomes an unexpected place: the children's hospital in downtown Chicago, where a giant humpback whale mama and her calf hang overhead from the lobby ceiling.

MRIs are Nolan's naptime. Medical tests are his play-time. The hospital hallways become Kevin's and my home gym—the place where we pace, wring our hands, cry our tears, pray our prayers, work out our fears, and beg God to bring us home. Eventually, spinal-cord surgery is the bedroom where he rests a while before waking to days of recovery, months of lying flat on his back, and years of in-home therapy.

Although we've been silently pleading for it, we are scared to leave our safe little surroundings at the hospital, the place with doctors and nurses and experts who know things and know how to do the right things related to spinal cords and babies. We, who are *definitively not* experts, know we have to face life outside of these walls sooner or later. So we bite our nails, pray some more, and tentatively say good-bye to our hospital home.

We return to our real-life house, only to find that a small tornado has blown through our street, blocked our front door, and taken our electricity with it. We feel powerless in more ways than one. Nolan's second home becomes a hotel where his big brothers swim in the pool and he, our champion, strives to recover.

When I was a child, my mom and dad moved around a lot—Dallas, Seattle, LA, Atlanta, and Oklahoma City—so for me, the concept of home has always been a series of streets and cities, losts and founds, packings and unpackings. At one of my favorite childhood homes, just a few days after we moved in, a hot-air balloon landed in our front yard. A picture of our house was in the newspaper, and I took that as a good omen; surely no one leaves a newsworthy address. But a few years later, we packed up once more.

If I have learned any lesson from my childhood of changing addresses, it's this: Lost is not necessarily when you don't know where you are; it's when you can't find your way back home.[5]

I tell my champion this story—about my various childhood houses and the hot-air balloon—as I look into his eyes and prop one of my legs over him to prevent him from rolling onto his tummy or crawling. We are back in our real-life house again, but he's not allowed to move for some time. His back is not ready or able or strong. These are our long, hard days at home.

But a year or so later, a light and easy day finally arrives. With the help of therapists and leg braces and family and big brothers and love and presence, Nolan takes his first steps. And all of us, this motley tribe of his, cry, snap pictures, and share the joy on social media. Nolan stumbles and giggles and falters and steadies himself again and again but never gives up. Our boy is indeed a champion.

And now—in the middle of our current pain and residual marriage imprecations because of it—nearly five years to the day since leaving his first home in that hospital, Kevin and I sit in the audience at Nolan's preschool graduation. He stands on a stage, without props or helps. He sings songs and recites verses about God's love. He is supposed to be serious through it all, but he loves to make people laugh, so instead he plays air guitar and air drums and yells, "Ooooh baby" loudly, all to his teacher's chagrin.

Nolan struts across the stage and graduates from preschool. Next year he will begin a new chapter, a new home of sorts: kindergarten. His days will be filled with bus rides and recess and homework and new friends, and me figuring out how to keep his life-threatening allergies in check, and eventually high school, then adulthood. But *one thing at a time*, I have to remind myself.

This morning I ask Nolan if remembers the whale in the hospital lobby, or his temporary home at the hotel. "Of course not, Mom! I've never lived in a hospital or a hotel! Mom! What are you even talking about?" he replies, laughably exasperated with my question. "I've always lived with you, Mama. I have always been at home with you."

After Nolan's graduation ceremony, his tribe once again cries and claps and cheers. He basks in our excitement and pride but has no idea the significance of it. I don't think he needs to understand the weight of it all quite yet. He is our five-year-old precious boy for now, and I want him to be five as long as he can.

I have always been at home with you, Mama.
Yes, I think, *that is true.*[6]

The night of Nolan's preschool graduation, there is a massive double rainbow in the sky. Moved by this tremendous mile marker for our boy, Kevin and I finally, really talk to each other. We name our anger. We name our pain. We talk about the infection in our relationship.

Our individual cups of lament at last begin to become one shared drink. We stop cursing imprecations at each other and finally work to get angry at the evil in this world, at the disappointment of illness, at the sadness of loss and grief. We champion each other. We begin to bring each other home again.

We don't agree on everything. We don't do it perfectly. We don't do it without losing our cool. But with the ongoing help of our "grief and life-change expert" counselor Mark, we decide that our goal is not constant agreement. Our goal is a mutual foundation of respect and support.

We begin to work on *the way* we have conflict because that matters as much as *what* we debate. During our sessions with Mark, we take time to listen to each other's laments, actively. We repeat them back to one another. We listen again.

I travel less and dig in locally at our church plant. We create a family calendar so that our schedules are no longer in competition. We begin to work together as a unit. We schedule regular date nights, times to recreate and play. Some are wins. Some aren't. But on our dates, we make some important discoveries. Kevin realizes that he needs adventure and Sabbath, and so begins an annual trek of the Colorado Trail. I remember that I love learning, so back to graduate school

I go. We empower each other to practice the work of self-care, soul-care—which matters during hard days. Slowly, we become an H again, next to each other, holding hands. Slowly, we uncover deep wounds, old wounds, old imprecations—and we help each other bandage them. Slowly, we bless each other in place of the old curses. And eventually, we clean the garage together, or Kevin cleans it when I'm in too much pain to do so. All of it, simple and basic. All of it love.

In her handbook on loss, author Anne Lamott writes, "Yet the gift of grief is incalculable, in giving you back to yourself."[7] For us, the gift of this season, as rough-and-tumble and imperfect as it's been, is that it's forced us to reexamine and reinvest in our marriage. I would never wish pain upon my children or my family. But without pain, without Nolan's issues and recovery, without my illness, we would have probably gone through marriage being *okay*. We would have gotten by. But our facade would have eventually crumbled to the ground. Thankfully, painful seasons don't allow for masquerading.

Kevin and I know that forgiveness is costly, and yet we choose to forgive and love each other again and again. I'm grateful to be doing this good, hard, healing work with him at my side and with God leading us.

If you're currently experiencing relational conflict, I can relate. I know how heartbreaking, draining, frustrating, and lonely-making it feels. For you, I am praying that God is especially near, answering your laments with his loving consolation. May you find strength to release your imprecations to him. May your relationships experience his healing.

Centuries after Jeremiah cried for his enemy to taste the

bitter cup of God's wrath, Jesus taught us to love our enemies. He even died for his enemies. Jesus took on all of the imprecations that live in our souls, all of the imprecations we deserve, and all of the imprecations in the world. He bore them; he became them; he swallowed them whole—and he overcame them.

If you feel alone in your relational conflict, rest assured. Jesus, your true champion, will continually carry you home.

A Psalm of Lament by David

LORD, do not rebuke me in your anger
    or discipline me in your wrath.
Your arrows have pierced me,
    and your hand has come down on me.
Because of your wrath there is no health
      in my body;
    there is no soundness in my bones
      because of my sin.
My guilt has overwhelmed me
    like a burden too heavy to bear. . . .

My back is filled with searing pain;
    there is no health in my body.
I am feeble and utterly crushed;
    I groan in anguish of heart.

All my longings lie open before you, Lord;
    my sighing is not hidden from you. . . .

> LORD, do not forsake me;
>> do not be far from me, my God.
> Come quickly to help me,
>> my Lord and my Savior.

PSALM 38:1-4, 7-9, 21-22

7

when
pain
is
chronic

SPRING AND SUMMER COME AND GO. Fall brings with
it the start of a new school year. I try my best to remain
actively involved with the boys all summer. But the moment
those gold, auburn, and orange leaves hit the ground,
and I find myself with free hours at home, I spend them
unproductively—on the couch.

I finally, officially, have a diagnosis: rheumatoid disease or
rheumatoid arthritis. Not osteoarthritis, as it's often confused
for, but rheumatoid, like old-school rheumatic fever. This
feels like an important distinction to me. Although I realize
it probably isn't. I just want people to understand—it's not

just that my elderly joints are wearing down, like my great grandma's. It's that my body tricks itself into believing that all 360 of its own joints are enemies. My body has turned Benedict Arnold.

The distinction matters because I want loved ones/acquaintances/strangers/Christian-Twitter-celebrities to know this is a *big deal*. Why? Well, truth be told, I'm a bit of a baby and I think I deserve a trophy for doing life with an illness.

When I tell someone new that I have an autoimmune disease, I feel as though I have to explain *myself* before I explain my diagnosis. I don't know why, but I want people to know that this isn't my fault. *Just so you know, I do Whole 30. I take fish oil. I ingest frankincense. But still, I have this thing called RA.*

That said, I actually sometimes wonder if I invited this. Have I unknowingly given myself a disease? Is this my fault? Or is this the tentacles of sin elongating outward, grabbing not only souls but our bodies as well?

Those of us with autoimmune issues are the anti-Spiderman. The venom flowing through Peter Parker's body empowers him with strength and gravity-defying agility. The venom flowing through ours simply disempowers. But people move on because we look okay. It's an imposition to ask friends to continue bringing meals day after day after day. How much longer can we justify paying someone else to clean the house? How much more care do we really need? So on top of the physical pain, we feel guilty for wanting help. We suffer in the worst possible way—silently.

When I gave birth, the amount of physical pain was

indescribable, but I always knew it was leading to something. The baby boys I felt kicking and squirming inside of me, the sons I'd been dreaming about, would arrive soon. *That* type of pain, *that* kind of suffering has meaning. Labor pain accomplishes something.

If you suffer from any lingering season of pain, you know the secret I know. Unlike productive labor pain, ongoing pain creates chaos. It lingers and leads nowhere. Persistent pain has no beginning and no end. Chronic suffering is like white noise, always on in the background of your life. And as Pastor J. Kevin Butcher writes in his beautiful book, *Choose and Choose Again*, "Truth be told, we've felt so little healing, so little love, that we struggle to pray, struggle to sing, and are desperate to know what to do next."[1]

Everyone fights some type of a chronic battle and struggles to know what next steps to take. My husband and other pastors I know often deal with the loneliness of leadership. My good friend Jaylynn is a grieving mom. There's Alwin, whose son is autistic, newly diagnosed. Sarah and Mark struggle with infertility. Jack's dad just died of cancer. Halley is dealing with self-confidence issues. Tristan is depressed. Jason lost his job. Michelle's husband died in a freak work accident. Ella is exhausted as a new mom. Caroline's house is under water, and the upkeep is draining all of her savings. Sharon's parents are ill. Dany's marriage is hanging on by a thread. Cynthia's husband walked out. Daniel's wife has early-onset Alzheimer's. Chloe's sister is still angry at her. The list, like chronic pain itself, goes on and on and on and on.

And all of us, no matter what we face, want to know that we aren't alone, that hope exists on the other side, that this isn't all some arbitrary joke life has decided to play on us. Ultimately, we want to know that our time in this wilderness will transform into a blooming, healing, beautiful, deep spiritual garden. We long to experience Jesus and the power of his resurrection here. But sometimes the process is slow. After all, it's hard to accept that we will never again be who we once were.

The Way Things Were

As I mentioned earlier, I spend a lot of time on the couch because my illness keeps me here. I get pneumonia, or a stiff neck, or a random fever. It hurts too much to walk upstairs. So I lie on the couch and waste my life away on social media.

I reluctantly join a Facebook group for graduates of my very small, very conservative high school. We laugh about the days we got into trouble at punk-rock concerts. We reminisce about the past. It's fun, initially, a bright spot in my day, to joke about old teachers and old music and old inside jokes. But I recall something I read once, that Facebook is a high-school reunion from hell.

No one on the Facebook page knows that I battle RA. Admitting my illness embarrasses me for some reason. Online, I get to be a pretend version of Aubrey. I like her. She has wit and charm and doesn't have to take injections every week or get hours' worth of transfusions. She doesn't have her blood drawn regularly.

As you may recall from chapter 3, faking is never helpful. Soon, the fake version of Aubrey mixes with the Facebook nostalgia. That's when I get weird.

It's as if the past twenty years in which I've married and mothered, ministered and matured no longer matter. The fifteen-year-old in me desperately wants the approval of my old high-school friends and acquaintances—the Facebook group's most successful people—The Chosen Ones. The Stars.

I start "liking" almost every comment the cool kids make, even if I disagree with them or find them unamusing. After a few days of this, I attempt to regain some semblance of real-life Aubrey, so I go back through the conversation threads and delete most of my comments. I un-like posts and memes I previously liked. But then *that* makes me feel insecure—*what if people think I'm wishy washy?*—so I re-like all over again.

Like I said, I get weird.

After a few days of this fickle behavior, I grow angry at myself. What am I doing? I'm lying on the couch in pain, obsessing over stupid social media, when I should take care of myself! I should work towards wellness! I should tend to my soul! Read my Bible! Listen to a positive podcast! Take Epsom-salt baths! I shouldn't do the actual opposite of self-care—get sucked into unreasonable high-school drama. Why am I giving Facebook this much power?

My heart gives a little warning sign, waves her little red flag. *Hey Aubrey*, she says, *get off social media. Spend a little time with me. Figure out what's going on in here.*

I call Kevin and ask him to pray for me. He's usually pretty good about dealing with my eccentricities, or at least he vowed to me on our wedding day that he'd stick with me through them, so he's stuck. He helps me laugh at myself in a way that gives perspective. His advice: "Step away from your screen. Now."

So I do. I remove myself from the group. (Which, admittedly, throws me into another round of anxiety. *What will they think of me now that I've left?* Not that anyone is paying me that much attention. No one thinks about me as much as I do.) I slam my laptop closed so harshly it nearly breaks.

But really, social media isn't the actual problem (though it sure does amplify it). The problem is that my disease has stolen so much of who I was and keeps me from so much of who I want to be. The problem, really, is that I can't stop fixating on my former glory.

The Glory of Mourning

Jeremiah spends a lot of Lamentations grieving Jerusalem's present pain in light of her past splendor. As he laments, Jeremiah looks backward: "In the days of her affliction and wandering Jerusalem remembers all the treasures that were hers in days of old" (1:7).

In other words, she, once great among nations, is now reduced to rubble and ash.

Again, I know my pain is minimal compared to the great suffering of the daughters and sons of Israel. But this, I realize, is the red flag my heart frantically waves. I've spent three decades as a follower of Jesus, but in these never-ending painful days, I've somehow forgotten to cling to my Savior. Instead, I cling to my former glory like one of those sad former high-school athletes who can't fathom getting rid of her trophies.

Sometimes affairs aren't with other people. Sometimes they occur with the fantasy version of oneself: *The Girl without Pain. The Girl from Before.* I wonder for probably the thousandth time where she'd be now. I'm frankly annoying myself with all this self-pity.

Haven't we all struggled with some version of a former-glory lament? For anyone walking through seasons of difficulty, particularly when that difficulty seems like it will never end, an inevitable part of the process is wondering about the what-ifs or the if-onlys.

In my ministry with women in overcoming shame and "not-enoughness," I've discovered that the healing process always involves a proactive journey of grief. The hurt little girl inside of each woman—*her* needs, *her* pain, the sadness in *her* heart—deserves to be voiced, honored, and lamented. A process of intentional grief helps us escape the prison of our pasts.

Similarly, in order to move through our pain, we need to create space to grieve our disrupted futures. In other words, we need to lament our what-could-have-beens. It's perfectly legitimate, healthy even, to grieve for past pain *and* for alternate versions of the future. Because our what-might-have-beens are very real losses.

Laments that look back are known by scholars as *laments of the dead*.[2] Aptly named, these laments grieve the death of another. These laments are often not even expressed directly to God, because the circumstances cannot be changed. There is nothing to actually ask of God. Still, they are laments that articulate the incomparable sadness of the loss of a loved one, the loss of someone who once belonged to you. These laments say good-bye to the past.

I think our former-glory or what-could-have-been laments are similar. They are an expression of looking backward—not so that we get stuck in the past or stumble over it, but as a way to surrender the past to God and begin living wholly in the new reality in front of us.

In our former-glory laments, we grieve for the life that "should" have been. Think of the lament of Hagar and little Ishmael in Genesis 21 for a moment. We see a glimpse of a former-glory lament here. Hagar and her boy were banished to the desert because of Sarah's jealousy. When they ran out of water, Hagar placed her little one under some bushes and sobbed, "I cannot watch the boy die" (verse 16).

In Hagar's lament, we see the pain of a mother watching her son suffer. This is not the existence this child was supposed to have. He should have been raised in the house of his father, Abraham. He should have been provided for. He should have known shelter, food, water, and family. He certainly should not be dying in the desert.

Thankfully, the Lord heard the cries of mother and son, stepped in, and provided water for them, a well in the desert. As Hagar said good-bye to what should have been, God stepped in and took Ishmael down another path altogether. Ishmael grew up to marry an Egyptian woman, became an archer in the desert, had many sons who became a great nation, and lived 137 years. God was always with him (Genesis 21:18, 20-21; 25:17). Though this was not the life that Hagar had initially envisioned for her son, it was still a meaningful life with God.

As we read Scriptures like these, it seems clear that when God hears our cries—even if they aren't directly spoken to him—he is moved to action. God never remains a passive listener. He is an involved God who wants our what-ifs. So one practical way to mourn our what-could-have-beens or our former glory is simply to note these feelings. Pay attention when a "what-if" is triggered. List them in a journal. Text them to a friend. Go back to your *hows*. Read them aloud to God. Some what-could-have-been ekahs might look like this:

- *How might our relationship have turned out differently if this conflict never occurred?*
- *If she were still here, how would my daughter have dressed up for Halloween? What costume would she have worn?*
- *How would my mom have responded if she could see me now?*
- *How would my husband have pitched in this Christmas?*
- *Had I tried this medical advice instead of the other, how might things have turned out?*

This work of looking back and acknowledging these painful what-ifs might initially cause some anxiety and agony. Doing this can, if we let it, become a way of trying to control the uncontrollable. In some cases, like mine, what-ifs can lead us down an ugly road of self-pity. However, they might also be the very laments that finally move you forward. They might also be the very laments that help open your eyes to see God's stream in your desert.

The Glory of Morning

The night of my Stepping Away from Facebook, I grab my lament journal from under the couch, where I've been stashing it for easy access. I write down some new ekahs, my chronic-pain/former-glory ekahs: *How do I learn to love this bitter, broken version of myself? How do I accept the unacceptable? How long, O Lord, will I look backward in resentment instead of looking upward in gratitude?*

I fall asleep on the couch, which I only realize because I wake up the next morning with a blanket over me, and my ekahs snug against my heart, tucked under the blanket.

It's early and the house is still silent, so I shuffle, quietly, from the couch to the kitchen in order to grab some coffee. I cringe at the effort it still takes just to walk a few feet.

I sit back down on the couch—my new home—and stare out the window at my neighbor's perfectly manicured backyard. My yard is a mess of wet, muddy leaves. But my neighbor somehow manages to have an Instagram-Perfect Pile of Fall Leaves, not to mention an antique rake, which leans idyllically against his restored red barn, *and* a thriving herb garden—in the backyard of all places, where no one can even see them! Okay, I'm jealous again. My neighbor is Isaac, tending to his picturesque existence. I'm Ishmael, sitting in stinky, stretched-out sweatpants on the couch.

I sit here trying not to be envious of my neighbor's photo-worthy life. I breathe in and out slowly, in order to live through the pain of lifting my coffee cup to my lips. In the middle of my reverie, my middle son sneaks downstairs in his pajamas and bare toes.

"Good morning, Mama." He whispers, so as not to wake up his brothers. "How do you feel today?"

Oh, the twang of guilt—how are my children processing my illness? I don't even know how to fathom that right now. (Note to self: Save money for my kids' future therapy bills.)

But being a kid, thankfully, he doesn't dwell too much on it, at least for right now. He flops on the couch next to me and snuggles in close. He begs me for screen time before school. I say no, of course. We burrow under the blanket, poke each other and giggle, and comment on the neighbor's self-important herb garden. *Should we sneak over and steal some for a morning omelet?* we wonder.

Our stomachs growl and we decide that we'd rather eat donuts than omelets. But we don't have donuts, so we settle for oatmeal. Kevin is still asleep. He's carried so much of the boys' needs lately, so I don't want to wake him. But to be honest, slow-cooking Irish oats feels like too big of an ordeal this morning. I force my body to walk back into the kitchen once more and grab some quick oats instead.

I light up the stove, pour in the water, and add the oatmeal. After it's cooked, Linc helps me pour the oatmeal into bowls. We add raw honey and organic blueberries and giggle some more as we sit down to eat our warm, sweet breakfast. And this moment, well, it's a delight, a grace, a taste of glory in the morning. I silently thank God for it.

After we finish eating, I get up from the table to take my pain meds. Soon my other boys wake up. The morning rushes on to school, to work for Kevin, to homework for the boys, to dinner, bath, and eventually to my bedtime on the couch once more.[3]

Throughout the day, though, I keep thinking about that moment in the morning. There on the couch and again at the kitchen table—with my coffee and oatmeal and my snuggly son—for that instant, I forgot my former-glory ekahs. For a brief moment, my thirst was quenched. I forgot the Facebook nonsense and the self-pity. For a brief moment, I felt free from the weight I've been carrying. For an instant, I moved from my hows to something new. Could a shift be occurring in my lament journey? A shift caused by the awareness of God's presence at work in my present?

I've stayed so focused on my what-might-have-beens, I've neglected to see how God is blessing me *now*—in and even through this pain. I've fixated on my former glory so much that I've missed out on what God is actually doing here. *This is what I need to learn to do*, I think. This is how I'll finally arrive at that elusive place called acceptance—by watching for, noting, gathering instances of hope and joy in one hand, even while wrestling with my darkest hours in the other. This truth rings loudly in my heart: Good and bad can exist at once. It's okay to admit that both things are true. My situation is hard *and* God has been good to me.

———•———

Before falling asleep, I kiss Kevin goodnight and he walks upstairs to our bedroom. Soon, I will feel well enough to join him, as my disease eventually, thankfully, enters remission. But for tonight, I fall asleep on the couch once more—this time, not writing down ekahs, but instead thinking about Jeremiah's own former-glory laments, his grief over the destruction of Jerusalem's Temple.

I recall something author Leslie Leyland Fields once wrote of the Israelites and of the temple: "They don't know yet that God came not to save his people *from* storm and suffering but to save them *through* storm and suffering. Israel *is* redeemed. The temple—Jesus himself—*is* restored."[4]

In my pain, I've forgotten that all of our storms and sufferings, all of our what-ifs are part of our redemption. As James says, when we face trials, we should consider it joy "because you know that the testing of your faith produces perseverance. Let perseverance finish its work so that you may be mature and complete, not lacking anything" (1:3-4).

So lament your social-media obsessions. Lament your days on the couch. Lament your former glories and all of those what-ifs. God wants them all. He wants every burden, every broken path, every looking back. But then, return your gaze to Jesus.

Listen for his voice, saying to you now, "Be strong and courageous, for I go with you—backward and forward, I will be there. I will never leave you nor forsake you—not now, not ever. I'm listening to your cries. I'm moving on your behalf. I'm here in this wilderness, providing a well in your what-ifs."

The Future Glory of Zion

"For a brief moment I abandoned you,
    but with deep compassion I will bring you back.
In a surge of anger
    I hid my face from you for a moment,
but with everlasting kindness

I will have compassion on you,"
says the LORD your Redeemer.

"To me this is like the days of Noah,
when I swore that the waters of Noah
would never again cover the earth.
So now I have sworn not to be angry with you,
never to rebuke you again.
Though the mountains be shaken
and the hills be removed,
yet my unfailing love for you will not be shaken
nor my covenant of peace be removed,"
says the LORD, who has compassion on you.

ISAIAH 54:7-10

8
learning
to
say
"yet"

I'M ALMOST FORTY WHEN my dad decides I should learn to drive a boat. While this isn't a survival skill—it's actually a privileged-first-world-person skill—Kevin, the boys, and I do enjoy time on the water. All I want out of life is a fabulous home with modern coastal flair, curated charm, and a stunning seascape. Is that too much to ask? My dad, unfortunately, doesn't have access to a seascape, nor does he know anything about modern flair. But Dad does have a small ski boat, which we love to borrow anytime he lets us. I'm excited to finally learn how to drive it.

Just before my sweet-sixteenth, my father taught me to

drive a car by setting a glass of wine in his lap and telling me not to spill the wine. In case you skimmed that, allow me to repeat. My dad PUT AN OPEN GLASS OF WINE in his lap and taught me to drive a car by saying, "Don't spill the wine. Be smooth. Be cool. Drive like you're on ice." He was like a jazzy Mr. Miyagi. (For those of you who just became anxious, don't fret. My dad is not an alcoholic; he's just a big fan of The Object Lesson. You should have seen him use a pair of cowboy boots to teach my sister and me about work ethic.) As a result of his totally insane—and, by the way, completely illegal—teaching methods, I can change traffic lanes with the grace of an Olympic ice dancer.

Dad's boat-driving lessons are different. I don't know if it's because I'm older or because he is, or that he'd never dare to stain his precious boat with a glass of red wine. But he no longer calmly Mr. Miyagis me. Mostly, he teaches me to drive his boat by repeating this mantra: "Don't panic. But panic."

"Watch for waves. Watch the water depth. Watch for other boats. Watch for potential tree trunks in the water. You don't need to panic but you also need to panic."

I take the "panic" part of his advice off the boat and into my soul. I make it my mantra. I try not to panic. But I panic. Although I can tell that something about my lament journey is shifting—I am not longer focusing so much on self-pity; I'm trying to be present; I'm seeing evidences of God's love—there is part of me that still lives in anticipation of the next tree trunk in the water.

It's been nearly three years since game change hit us—three years since I got sick, since Cameron died, since Nolan was in recovery. But because it all happened almost simultaneously, I keep expecting something like that season to hit again. I keep waiting for the next bottom to drop out, and it causes me some anxiety.

My mom, on the other hand, is not a panicky person. When she prays, she calls God *El Roi*, the God who sees. Mom says she's never prayed a prayer to El Roi that wasn't answered, never lost something that wasn't found, never looked for something that wasn't revealed, never worried about something she's left in his care. "His eyes are not shut," she reminds me. "He isn't asleep, unaware of all the circumstances. He sees."[1]

Even though my pain and grief are not the gaping wounds they were even a few months ago, they are still tender. I still haven't felt the presence of God in a long time. I haven't experienced his nearness in a long while. Underneath my panic, I just really miss Jesus.

El Roi, I write in my ekah journal, *let me rest and trust that even if I can't feel you, you see me.*

Presence

When I was a junior-high ministry pastor, winter camp was a staple of our calendar year. Each Saturday night of camp, as we prepared to say good-byes, the students would sob. I mean, they'd bawl their precious little tween eyes out.

I confess that I didn't have a lot of patience for this. To me, the kids appeared to have been emotionally manipulated, or were just overtired from all of the camp's activities. They couldn't possibly be expressing sincere sadness.

Looking back now, I wonder if, in their messy adolescent

way—without shame or cynicism—this was an early form of lament. At camp, these students experienced beauty, hope, healing, community, love, fun, worship, and the wonder of God. They felt the Spirit, the presence of God with them. Perhaps they were truly, authentically lamenting the loss. Whenever we experience a sense of God's presence, that experience powerfully strengthens, reassures, comforts, and heals us. I recently heard a pastor say, "No experience on earth is a substitute for a personal encounter with God's presence." But the apparent loss of his presence? Well, it's downright devastating.

When Jesus' presence seems absent in the midst of my panic, I find that canned spiritual answers and my usual spiritual disciplines, things that once helped me feel connected to him, no longer work. So one day, I try a new spiritual practice, something I read about in a book. Each morning, I stretch out on the floor of my closet, lie there quietly, and will my mind to stop panicking. I remind myself to breathe in and out slowly, to practice gratefulness, peacefulness, and presentness. But I find that instead of being still, I end up trying really freaking hard to be grateful and peaceful and present. Mostly, I feel like the bull and God's presence is the china shop.

Of grieving his wife, Joy, C. S. Lewis wrote, "You are like the drowning man who can't be helped because he clutches and grabs. Perhaps your own reiterated cries deafen you to the voice you hoped to hear. . . . Perhaps your own passion temporarily destroys the capacity."[2]

Have I incapacitated myself from knowing God's presence

because I'm so frantic to lament correctly? Is El Roi choosing not to see me because I'm doing something wrong?

I strain to connect with God, attempt to worship him, try to feel him, but mostly I just thrash around. After a few more attempts at "the closet floor," I realize it's not cutting it. So I decide to meet with a spiritual director from my graduate-school program. The Christian life is meant to be lived in community, not privately. I can't do this on my own.

When we meet, she reads Psalm 22 over me, the same words that Jesus lamented on the cross—"My God, my God, why have you forsaken me? Why are you so far from saving me, so far from my cries of anguish?" (verse 1).

"What did Jesus do on the cross?" she asks me. "And don't get super theological here," she adds. "I am not looking for the 'right' answer."

I think for a moment. Jesus thirsted. He lamented. He talked to his neighbor. He prayed.

"He embraced his limitedness," my wise spiritual director adds. "He lamented that he didn't feel God's presence and couldn't do anything about it. In our own suffering, we don't have to do much more than that. Part of the reason you're panicking is because you're trying too hard to control the outcome of lament. You're trying to be limitless. Just let go. Just let him save you."

At another meeting, after I tell her that I still can't feel God's presence, she asks me this: "When, in the past, have you felt God's presence?"

For a moment, my old friend Panic creeps in. *Have I ever felt God's presence? Am I even a Christian? Is God even real?*

She senses my anxiety.

"Don't worry," she says softly. "Let's be silent a moment and ask God's Spirit to meet us here in this question."

In the silence, I think of just a few of the many times I've felt God's presence over the years: when I was baptized at age eleven; the first time I prayed with someone who wanted to follow Jesus; when, stuck in the darkness of shame from my past, God led me down a healing journey; while learning from the Zambian people; recently, in graduate school; when my children were born; on my wedding day; even just sitting outside, feeling a gentle breeze, hearing a birdsong, seeing a butterfly—all of which have felt like God's kind presence.

I can't put my finger on why or how, but in those moments, I knew God was with me. Sometimes it was discovering just the right Bible verse to calm my fears. Other times, I experienced great joy. At still other moments, his presence came in the form of conviction for sin and the freedom of repentance, or a sense that nothing else mattered but Jesus and his power and glory, or an image of God's love.

"You'd be surprised at how different everyone's experience of God's presence is," she says. "But the thread I see through them all, the common theme, is this: grace. Anytime we experience God's presence, it's never because we *did* anything. It's because God's grace opens up the veil."

Tears are burning down my cheeks because I know she's right.

I've tried so hard to say the right incantation, the perfect ekah. I've driven myself crazy trying to impose my will on God's. I've ricocheted back and forth between *panic* and *don't panic*. I've tried my best to force God to obey me—to heal my sickness, to bring back Cameron, to make Nolan okay, to help me travel back in time so that none of this ever even began. But in so doing, I've put myself in the place of God.

I've adopted a sinful attitude of "I need to forgive God for betraying me." Like the night of the choir concert, which now feels so long ago, when I realized I felt like God had disappointed me. But, really, I've not trusted him. I've refused to rest in him.

[My Repentant lament, at long last, begins. *I'm so sorry, God. Please forgive me. I want to turn away from my selfishness and return to worshiping and placing my faith in you.*]

God's presence is not anything we achieve through sheer willpower and determination. We can't force his hand. We must attend to and be open to God's presence, certainly. If we ignore him, or refuse to open ourselves, our schedules, our seasons, our whole hearts to God, we'll miss out on the benefits, treasures, and spiritual blessings granted to us in Jesus. But here's the point: God's grace greets and transforms *us*, whether or not we deserve it. And it's in believing that, in choosing to trust even when it feels like we have no reason to, that we take a powerful step forward in our lament.

The Mystery of Vav

Let's take another look at Lamentations. In the structure of Lamentations, Jeremiah crafted an image of the city of Jerusalem, a picture of its rise and fall, and a mirror of his own lament journey. The book of Lamentations, visually, looks like this:

		Chapter 3: 66 verses		
Chapter 1: 22 verses	Chapter 2: 22 verses		Chapter 4: 22 verses	Chapter 5: 22 verses

As you can see, chapter 3—the center of Jeremiah's lament—is also the longest/highest chapter. But when we get to chapters 4 and 5, Jeremiah's structure begins to break down—an image of Jerusalem's downfall, and an image of Jeremiah himself, exhausted from suffering.

I recognize that I'm kind of nerding out right now, so bear with me. As I look at that image above, I can't help but wonder if something about chapter 3 is important. Why else would Jeremiah take us on a such a high climb? Here's what I think: Chapter 3 is both the physical and emotional climax of Lamentations. It is the heart of Jeremiah's lament. It is the very moment that the prophet's cry is most personal and passionate. And just before he seems to give up—something significant happens. Here in chapter 3, verse 21, Jeremiah crosses the mysterious line of *vav*, the sixth letter of the Hebrew alphabet.[3]

The letter *vav*, interestingly, is shaped like a little nail, a straight up and down line, or a single downward stroke. It is known as the hook, or tent-peg letter. This cannot be coincidental. Here, in the heart of his lament, at the very moment of vav, Jeremiah hammers his stake into the ground. "Yet this I call to mind and therefore I have hope," declares Jeremiah. "Because of the LORD's great love we are not consumed, for his compassions never fail. They are new every morning; great is your faithfulness" (3:21-23).

As he crosses vav, Jeremiah utters the most powerful word in all of Lamentations: *yet*.

Yet is the moment the prophet moves from his painful ekahs to his only hope. *Yet* is the driving point, the firm foundation, the stake-in-the-ground of all laments. *Yet* is the hope of God's loving presence—even when we can't feel him.

Jeremiah's *yet* is found in the unchanging, steadfast love of God. Through his *yet*, Jeremiah declares, "Even if this suffering never ends, I will always worship God."

Yet is the paradigm shift of all laments. *Yet* arises even when the cancer isn't cured, when the debt never decreases, when the boyfriend doesn't call, when the child continues to struggle, when the questions aren't answered, when the loved one hurts you again. *Yet* believes that even if it doesn't go well with you, Jesus is still enough. His compassionate love is more than enough. "[Yet] is a praise that can now hope all things, having been forced to let go of everything," writes musician Michael Card.[4]

Yet is the fighter's prize. *Yet* is the hard-won faith. *Yet* hopes in God, for God's sake alone.

"In the darkness we have a choice that is not really there in better times," writes Pastor Timothy Keller in his treatise on grief and suffering. "We can choose to serve God just because he is God. . . . If we do that—we are finally learning to love God for himself, and not for his benefits."[5]

All laments lead to the truest form of worship—the worship of God alone. Not God and blessings, not God and benefits, but God for God's sake. No matter what happens. No matter how violently the storm rages. No matter God's apparent absence. Lament keeps on. Lament utters a profound *yet*: "This is horrible. Yet I will praise my God, for he alone is worthy."

I've known that the goal of lament is *not* fast-acting pain removal. But thinking over my spiritual director's words about God's grace, and over Jeremiah's vav, I realize something else. Lament *is* the art of trusting God no matter what he gives, no matter what he takes.

Suffering, if we let it, can birth genuine faith. Our *yet* in lament adopts the attitude of Lamentations 3: "Who can speak and have it happen if the Lord has not decreed it? Is it not from the mouth of the Most High that both calamities and good things come?" (3:37-38).

Keep Up Your Courage

After my spiritual-direction session that day, I sit in my car in the office parking lot, pull out my phone, and open up the Bible app. I reread some Scriptures I've been thinking about a lot lately—from Acts 27, the story of Paul's sail to Rome.

A hurricane comes. The Bible calls it a "nor'easter" (Acts 27:14, MSG). Paul and the other sailors take such a violent battering from the storm, they are forced to throw their cargo overboard. The crew has to tie ropes under the ship just to keep it intact. Acts 27:20 reports, "When neither sun nor stars appeared for many days and the storm continued raging, we [Paul and his crew] finally gave up all hope of being saved."

Yet in the middle of the darkness and storm, Paul has a dream. An angel of God reassures Paul that he and all the sailors will survive. "So keep up your courage, men," Paul announces to his suffering sailors, "for I have faith in God that it will happen just as he told me" (Acts 27:25).

Through the nor'easter, I will sail with you, God tells Paul. *I will carry you through. Have courage.*

I think once more about Jesus on the cross, about Paul in his hurricane, and even about my dad and me wavering between our panic/don't panic. In all scenarios, the waters are rough—*yet* we can keep up our courage, we can have hope, because we do not sail the stormy seas alone.

This is our firm foundation in disequilibrium—a God so intimately intertwined with suffering that he transforms the very nature of suffering itself. Jesus gives us a new *way* to suffer. Christians can suffer with *yet*-attitudes—we can cross the line of vav—because we go through life with God as our faithful captain.

Think of Jeremiah's life. The weeping prophet suffered deeply. The people he was called to serve treated him terribly. They vehemently opposed his words. They plotted to kill him (Jeremiah 11:18-19). He experienced ridicule (Jeremiah 20:7) and imprisonment (Jeremiah 32:2). He was called a liar. He was even kidnapped (Jeremiah 43:4-6). Jeremiah's ministry was not dotted with accolades, achievements, or a growing platform. It was marked by misery. Still, Jeremiah put his stake in the ground—for no other reason than the Lord's great love.

We tend to assume that God's calling will equal our happiness or success or freely opened doors, but sometimes we walk through overwhelming situations and God says, "Hey, don't panic, because this difficult place is precisely where I am going to meet you and reveal myself to you. This is where you will learn the true meaning of *yet*."

I put my phone down, pull my ekah journal out of my purse, and write this: *I want to love you no matter what. Help me when my faith falters. When I can't feel you, help me to keep my stake in the ground—held there by your love.*

Over time, I notice that my ekah journal changes. Whereas before I prayed only for God to rescue me, I start to praise him for being my great Rescuer. Before, I begged God to help me. Now, I thank him for being my Helper. I begin to sense Jesus with me again, and I'm so grateful.

Of course, it's good to ask God for rescue and help— that's a crucial part of lament and an important part of our intimacy with God. But thankfully, laments aren't stagnant. As God's grace and presence shift our paradigms, our laments shift to *yet*.

Friend, God may feel absent. But truthfully, he sees you. He is carrying you through every storm.

A Lament by Jeremiah

He pierced my heart
    with arrows from his quiver.
I became the laughingstock of all my people;
    they mock me in song all day long.
He has filled me with bitter herbs
    and given me gall to drink.

He has broken my teeth with gravel;
    he has trampled me in the dust.
I have been deprived of peace;

I have forgotten what prosperity is.
So I say, "My splendor is gone
    and all that I had hoped from the LORD."

I remember my affliction and my wandering,
    the bitterness and the gall.
I well remember them,
    and my soul is downcast within me.
Yet this I call to mind
    and therefore I have hope:

Because of the LORD's great love we are not consumed,
    for his compassions never fail.
They are new every morning;
    great is your faithfulness.
I say to myself, "The LORD is my portion;
    therefore I will wait for him."

LAMENTATIONS 3:13-24

with

Mitchel's Lament

MITCHEL AND HIS WIFE, Sarah, are dear friends of ours and longtime partners in ministry. In my humble opinion, Mitchel is one of the best communicators in the world. He pastors a massive multiethnic congregation in Maryland. I asked Mitchel to share a lament because I respect him tremendously and because he has known pain and grief—and walked with many through their own suffering. I have no doubt you'll be blessed by his words.

Mitchel

I'm not good at lament. My first response is to try to fix what is wrong. I listen with a problem-solving mind-set, acquire the relevant data, and then attempt to "rescue" the suffering person. I might initially offer a consoling word, but then I'm all business.

Compassion? Empathy? I've been at it long enough that I can demonstrate both while still trying to help find a way forward. It wasn't until I was faced with formidable tragedies and grave injustices in my pastoral journey that I began to learn what it means to lament.

How do you problem-solve when a church member loses his young-adult son to homicide? Or when a dear friend receives citizenship into "cancer land"? What can you do when a friend runs face-first into a racism wall that no one saw?

Any attempt to fix would be naive or, at worst, an empty promise. Explanations can seem empty and insensitive. We all know how Christian clichés such as "God has a greater good" can feel. The only biblically appropriate response is lament—to sit in the aftermath of what has happened and to cry out to God together. Sometimes I've needed to lament on behalf of the person who has no more strength to cry. It might be a long lament over dinner. It might happen in a hallway embrace as the news of a sudden loss is shared for the first time.

In walking with people through grief and loss, I've recognized how powerless I am to rescue anyone. And I've been surprised (and humbled a bit) to discover that people rarely look to me for rescuing. Rather, they're desiring to connect, to be validated that their suffering or the injustice they are facing hasn't somehow disqualified them from personhood. They're not even coming for answers—they just want to be reminded that God hasn't forgotten them. So we lament together. We do so not in a cynical, hopeless sorrow, but in ambidextrous lament—the promises of the presence and character of God in one hand and the real, hard, bitter hardship in the other.

As I think about the three life situations that seem to incite lament the most—injustice, inexplicable tragedy, and serious illness—I am learning that powerful people do not know how to lament. They're used to being able to affect a situation, leveraging their power for their own benefit or someone else's. People in control don't need lament because lament is for the helpless, the weak—those who have no advocate or way forward but for the mercy of God.

Recently, I was having lunch with a college student whose father was a prayer partner of mine. I say "was" because he died in an unexpected and incredibly tragic way. I lost my own father not more than a year ago, so she and I had a prolonged time of comparing notes. I asked her about some of the more boneheaded things people had said to her over the course of the visitation and funeral. (There were lots.) As we shared our common grief journey, we came up with a picture of an old-school balance scale where the weight of one thing is compared to the other. The death of her father was on one side, an extremely heavy, hard, sucky tragedy. And it was as if every encouraging comment was almost an attempt to balance out the scale. "Look at all the people who will hear the gospel." "The fruit of his ministry is incredible." Each time we try to balance out grief, we flex our power. We think that if we can somehow help her see the good (by the power of our words and insight), then she'll be comforted and we'll have done some good. It's about us, not the person grieving.

When I am with someone in lament, we are saying together, "God, you're the only audience we want right now. You're our only hope." There's no explanation that can balance out this loss. It's the echo of Psalm 13—"How long, LORD . . . ?" How long will this continue? How long will this case be unresolved? How long will the sadness oppress? How much can a person bear? Together, we long and plead for God to put his hand on the other side of that scale and press to make it equal. We do it together because we're all too easily sucked into trusting our own power or being hopelessly overwhelmed by what we see or are told. In lament together, we're reminded that the powerlessness we feel is valid, and we cry out to the only one who can and will dry every tear, wipe every eye, heal every sickness, and reunite every lost one.

9
when you just need to do something

Handholds in the
Days of Doubt

I FIRST RESPOND TO THE GOSPEL at age eleven, at an old-fashioned revival meetin' in my Oklahoma City Southern Baptist church. I walk down the aisle and tell the preacher that I am a sinner in need of a Savior, and I give my life to Christ that very day. I immediately get baptized and begin diving into the Bible, prayer, and a life of discipleship. I love Jesus. I experience him through his Word mostly, but also through little, special things—like butterflies.

In my childlike, unquestioning, undoubting faith, every time I see a butterfly I believe it is a gift from God—meant just for me. I wear butterfly earrings and butterfly hairclips and hang postcards of butterflies all over my bedroom wall. Every butterfly is a sign that God loves me deeply.

In my lamenting, I've forgotten some of the childlike ways in which I once interacted with God. There hasn't been much space for an uncomplicated faith over the past several years, and I long for that again. Don't you?

One night, I tell this to some of our church-planting friends, over tacos—not about the butterflies, but about my longing for a childlike experience of God again. These are friends who've walked a lament journey themselves— a heartbreaking sudden job loss, a painful career change. Now they are part of a thriving, multiplying church-plant ministry. But it was quite a road to get there. They are incredible people.

One of our friends responds, "What if you started a child-like spiritual practice?"

"What do you mean?" I ask.

"What if, for the next thirty days, you ask God to make himself real to you? Each morning, pray something like, 'God, make yourself real to me, like you did when I was young.' What if you boldly asked for that? I wonder how he would show up."

I wonder too. For the first time in years, I decide to be brave and lay out a fleece. I dare God to answer me. I've been so afraid to do this, so afraid he'll fail to answer. But I have more strength now than I did even a few months ago, more courage in Christ. So I try this suggested practice. What I don't tell our friends, or Kevin, or anyone is that I begin to pray that childlike prayer—with the specific request that God will meet me through butterflies again.

There's no easy road through lament, no simple steps to get from *how* to *yet*. I'd love to tell you that if you start an ekah journal, lament to God, and count 1-2-3, all confusing emotions about your situation will fly away like a butterfly.

If you feel stuck in the darkness, it can help to have handholds, some fleeces of your own, that will remind you of God's presence and faithfulness—that will strengthen your heart and take you back to your childlike wonder and faith.

Just as my friend invited me into a prayer practice, I'd like to invite you into a couple of spiritual practices as well. They just might be a handhold for you during your own trials.

Practices of Seeing More

If you've set foot on the earth, you've suffered. Or you've walked with someone who has gone through *something*— a difficult childhood, a job loss, financial woes, a painful relationship, tragedy, injury, illness, addiction, a door closed, marriage struggles, prodigal children, hurtful parents. The hard things that come our way can feel never-ending. That's probably how the disciples felt in Mark 4:35-41, one the most popular passages of Scripture when it comes to storms of life:

> That day when evening came, he said to his
> disciples, "Let us go over to the other side." Leaving
> the crowd behind, they took him along, just as he
> was, in the boat. There were also other boats with
> him. A furious squall came up, and the waves broke

over the boat, so that it was nearly swamped. Jesus was in the stern, sleeping on a cushion. The disciples woke him and said to him, "Teacher, don't you care if we drown?"

He got up, rebuked the wind and said to the waves, "Quiet! Be still!" Then the wind died down and it was completely calm.

He said to his disciples, "Why are you so afraid? Do you still have no faith?"

They were terrified and asked each other, "Who is this? Even the wind and the waves obey him!"

These verses pay tribute to our very human plight of pain, struggle, and doubt in the midst of very real, very scary storms of life. Which likely made the book of Mark particularly resonant among suffering Christians in Rome.

I imagine that this story—of their Savior in a storm—would have spoken powerfully to them.

Jesus went on that boat "just as he was," wrote Mark—a descriptor I find myself pausing over, rereading, meditating on again and again. Why, I wonder, did Mark feel the need to include that detail? *Jesus, just as he was.*

In ancient tales, great heroes of old often call on the name of gods for protection. They pray in the name of someone or something. Even Jonah, in a similar situation to that of Jesus in the boat, is urged by the sailors to pray in the name of his God.[1] But in this storm, Jesus simply rises and speaks: "quiet" to the wind, "be still" to the waves.

Jesus calls on the name of no one. Why?

Is it because his is the name above all names?

Jesus *just as he was*—no magic help, no tricks up his sleeve, no facades—fully human and yet fully something other—wields the same power that created the world.

Jesus is the same God in Genesis, whose Spirit hovered over the chaos and darkness of the waters and spoke, bringing about order, light, and life. Jesus is the same God who parted the Red Sea in Exodus. Jesus is the same God the psalmists describe as being in control over the raging water.[2] Jesus is the same God who kept Jonah alive in the belly of a whale. He, alone, has ultimate authority over the forces of evil, chaos, and storms in this world.

Jesus has borne the worst of storms for you. On the cross, the emotional, physical, and spiritual waters raged around him. But he battled on and beat them down—motivated by his unfathomable ocean of love for you.

But what does any of this have to do with seeing the bigger picture? How does this relate to spiritual practice?

In times of struggle, God invites us to remember—again and again—that he is the same God from Mark 4. Jesus has power and authority over your storm because he has power over every storm. We know this, but we don't always feel it. We can't hold it in our hands. And so we need a way to *practice* it, to bring it to life in our real days, morning, noon, and night.

The 5 Rs

One practice that helps me see more involves 5 Rs—reading, reacting, rehearsing, receiving, and responding to God's Word. These 5 Rs are a "slow down" method of Bible study, a simple way to interact with God's Word.

If you don't already have one, get yourself a journal or a Bible in which you can take notes. If you're more visually inclined, grab an artist's Bible with room in the margins for pictures. Then practice the 5 Rs, which looks a little something like this:

First, thank the Holy Spirit for being with you. Ask God's Spirit to guide your time, help you discern his voice, and assist you in tuning your awareness to God's presence. Then:

- **Read** the Scripture. Use Mark 4 or any of the lament verses I've provided for you throughout the text. I've also included some verses at the end of this book in appendix B.
- **React**. What are your initial thoughts about this passage? What words, images, or questions come to mind as you read? Don't judge yourself. Just notice and jot down things that cross your mind.
- **Rehearse**, which comes from an old Anglo-French phrase meaning "to go over again, . . . to rake over, turn over."[3] Read the Scriptures again, this time aloud, and note any repeating words or phrases. Pay attention for themes. Observe what else is happening around those Scriptures. What might God be saying about himself here?
- **Receive**, asking God what he wants you to hear. Stay quiet, attentive. Listen for his still, small voice. Pay attention for an image, word, verse, or any thought that he brings to mind. Wait patiently. If you don't hear anything, that's okay. Just tell him that and keep going.

- **Respond** by writing, drawing, or creating a prayer (of lament, if you'd like) based on your reading.

When we're in the thick of something painful, we often need some guidance, someone to take our hand and show us where to go when we're too overwhelmed with grief to figure it out ourselves. The point of the 5 Rs is to help us slow down, marinate in God's presence, and listen for his still, small voice.

No matter what rages, keep clinging to his Word. Keep practicing.

Reawakening the Imagination[4]

In our hard moments, if we're not careful, our minds and hearts can easily become filled with distorted images of God. We can start to believe lies: *God is not good. God is unloving. God is unfair. God is a harsh, patriarchal Father-figure.** The point is, if we aren't paying attention, we can begin to believe, like the disciples in the storm, that God has abandoned us.

"The best way to bring healing to the soul," writes Dr. Rick Richardson, "is to let the Spirit of God work in our mental symbols, memories and imagination. . . . Our imagination gives us access to our most painful, anxious experiences and feelings in a way that allows *objectivity* in the healing process."[5]

What if we began to invite God to reawaken our imaginations—our minds, our hearts, our souls, our creative

---

* Throughout this book, I refer to God as "he" or "him" because I personally relate to God as a loving daddy, just as Jesus did. But I know this image of God as singularly male may not fit your theological point of view. And for others, especially if you've had a painful experience with men or with earthly fathers, this concept can be a real struggle. If that's you, I'm lamenting with you and praying that God would heal your heart with his *Abba* (daddy) love.

centers—to the truth of who he actually is? What if we asked him to replace our distorted images of him with complete and beautiful images? As Richardson asserts in his book *Experiencing Healing Prayer*, if we do that, *then* we will begin to experience spiritual healing.[6]

Therein lies the heart of the practice of reawakening the imagination, which looks something like this:

Imagination

1. Set aside some quiet time. Go for a walk in nature. Or if you're indoorsy (like me), dim the lights and light a candle.
2. Spend time thanking God for his presence. Then ask God to bring to mind any unbiblical or untrue images you have of him.
3. Ask God to replace those false images with ones that are true. Don't overthink this. Don't be hard on yourself. Be patient and expectant for God to reveal an image of himself. Search the Scriptures for descriptors of God. Ask God to help you internalize those descriptors.
4. If this isn't working, invite a prayer partner into the process with you. She or he might have a word for you from God or be able to confirm the images or words you receive. Prayer is often more powerful with another person, since where two or more are gathered, God is there (Matthew 18:20).
5. Whatever image or word you receive, praise God for it. Spend some time considering it. Ask God to help you discern what it means, how he wants you to grow from it.

As I have practiced reawakening the imagination, I've learned that I don't have an amazing prophetic gift like some women and men in my life who regularly receive images from God. Mostly, I look for images and wind up seeing the inside of my eyelids.

But one day, God gave me the image of a swimming lion. Through that image, I realized God was calling me deeper into his presence, to dive deep into the ocean of grace with him. He was tenderly waiting just under the surface while I wrestled with my pain and waded in shallow waters.

My swimming lion was a profoundly healing image. Struggling to find my sea legs in the murky waters of suffering, I sensed God telling me that I didn't need to find my sea legs on my own; I just needed to rest on his back. He'd swim for me.

Now, each morning, I try to imagine myself swimming with the lion, or resting on his back, or snuggling against his warm fur, resting in his giant paws. This image of God has reawakened my imagination to his fierce and tender presence.

Take time to ask God for a fresh vision of who he is. It may not come immediately. (You might spend some time staring at your eyelids, like me.) But I believe his response will come, and you'll be amazed at his personal care for you.

Keep reawakening that imagination of yours. Keep reading God's Word with the 5 Rs in mind.

Whatever spiritual practices you choose, keep repeating them until hope arrives.

———•♦•———

I'm only a few days into my recent practice of praying that God will show up somehow through a butterfly. I'm attending some of our friends' church-plant opening, celebrating with them. After the service I stand by the entrance, putting on my coat, preparing to leave. A woman I've never met almost tackles me. "Oh, phew," she says. "I've been looking all over for you. I am so glad you didn't leave yet!"

I look at her curiously and assume it's her job to get visitors plugged into the church. I start to tell her that she doesn't need to get my information. "I'm a church planter myself, just here to celebrate my friends, not here to join the church. But thanks. I don't need to fill out any visi—."

She cuts me off. "Oh no. That's not it."

"Okay?" I reply, as a question.

She goes on, "So you might think I'm weird because we don't know each other. But I was sitting behind you in the service and sometimes I get these little visions from God. I don't know what you think of this." She pauses. Then she continues, "I want you to know that God kept giving me a very clear image for you. I kept seeing a butterfly."

I gasp. My eyes immediately fill with tears.

"Have you been going through something difficult?" she asks.

"Why?" I ask, not wanting to give anything away.

"Well, the butterfly is not quite out of its cocoon yet. Its wings are wet and wilted. God was telling me to tell you that these wet and wilted days, these days when you feel so trapped, are a necessary part of this season. He has something new for you, something *next* for you, but you are meant to go through this stage before you can fully fly." She grabs my hands and looks intently into my eyes, waiting for my reaction. "Does any of that mean anything to you?" she asks.

I can barely get a word out. I just hug her, whisper a thank-you, and run to my car. I climb in the front seat and bawl like a little girl.

"You see me, God! You do! You do! Thank you! Thank you! Thank you!" I cry. I can't even believe God's kindness—the specificity of his answer to my butterfly prayer, his personal words about this journey.

In lament, we ask God our doubtful questions: Do you see me? Do you hear me? Are you real? God never chides us for asking. Instead, he always answers with a resounding, mind-blowing *Yes. I am good, my little one. I see you. I hear you. I love you. Trust me. Know me. Even in your pain.*

God is with you, even when you can't muster the strength to find him.

He is transforming this wet, wilted season of yours—and if you let him, transforming *you* in the midst of it.

Jonah's Lament

In my distress I called to the LORD,
    and he answered me.
From deep in the realm of the dead I called for help,
    and you listened to my cry.
You hurled me into the depths,
      into the very heart of the seas,
      and the currents swirled about me;
all your waves and breakers
    swept over me.
I said, "I have been banished

from your sight;
yet I will look again
   toward your holy temple."
The engulfing waters threatened me,
   the deep surrounded me;
   seaweed was wrapped around my head.
To the roots of the mountains I sank down;
   the earth beneath barred me in forever.
But you, LORD my God,
   brought my life up from the pit.
When my life was ebbing away,
   I remembered you, LORD,
and my prayer rose to you,
   to your holy temple.

Those who cling to worthless idols
   turn away from God's love for them.
But I, with shouts of grateful praise,
   will sacrifice to you.
What I have vowed I will make good.
   I will say, "Salvation comes from the LORD."

JONAH 2:2-9

10

beyond yourself

Lament Loves
Company

MY GRANDMOTHER, affectionately known as "Memaw," has a heart attack. I jump on a plane to Oklahoma and head to her hospital bedside.

One of our oldest family friends, Theresa, greets me at the door with a warm hug and says, "Oh, Aubrey! Let me look at your hands. My husband, John, used to always say, 'Aubrey has the most beautiful hands. Farrah Fawcett hands. Piano-player hands.'"

One spring break, when I was thirteen years old, I stayed at Theresa's beach house. She told me that angels lived in her home. They visited and chatted with her. The thought

hope can/voiceless

of angels—even good angels with halos and harps—in this house where I was eating breakfast burritos, swimming in the pool, and playing dominos each night really, *really* freaked me out. I couldn't sleep. I was so anxious about angels watching over me, *spying on me.*

One evening, I snuck out of the guest room around midnight to look for a Bible, hoping to find some solace in the words of God. I found one in the kitchen, but wanting to avoid a run-in with any household angels, I bolted back to the guest room. Once I was snuggled protectively under my bedcovers, I searched through the pages of the Bible for a verse—something to calm my anxious heart. But I couldn't seem to find what I was looking for. (This was before phone apps, so the "Holy Bible" app didn't exist yet. I'm old. Shut up.)

Without warning, the pages of the Bible began to turn *by themselves*. I looked up. There was no fan above me. I looked around—no air-conditioning unit blasting. Yet the pages of my Bible were literally moving.

Just as suddenly as they started, they stopped.

I looked down. There at the top of the page was the perfect verse, words to comfort me, words to help me rest. The precise words I needed to calm my fears and help me sleep: "When you lie down, you will not be afraid; when you lie down, your sleep will be sweet. Have no fear of sudden disaster or of the ruin that overtakes the wicked, for the LORD will be at your side and will keep your foot from being snared" (Proverbs 3:24-26).

Perhaps one of the angels moved the page, or perhaps Jesus was with me then, as he is with me now in this hospital, as I sheepishly slide my hands back in my pockets. They don't look like graceful piano-player hands anymore. Now veins pop out of my skin like prairie-dog tunnels. My fingers resemble sausages.

"They used to be pretty," I say.

But now I have RA. Sigh.

Ewwww. I stop myself in my self-absorbed tracks. This is just getting gross. My precious Memaw is near death. Theresa isn't even really talking about me. She is grieving the recent loss of her husband, her partner of sixty years, and just wants to talk about him. And all I can think about are my former Farrah Fawcett hands. Clearly, something in this self-absorbed heart of mine needs renewing.

To Lament Is to Love

All laments tend to start self-focused (my will, my problem, my questions of God; *Where is he?*). But as we surrender our pain to him, God shifts our focus so that we begin to look God-ward (thy will, thy goodness, thy purpose, thy sovereignty). But lament journeys don't stop there. Lament should also lead *other-ward*. God never rescues us from suffering solely for our sake. God's healing work in our lives is always meant to benefit others.

When injustice exists, when friends and family members grieve and suffer, when neighbors are being oppressed and fearing for their lives, perhaps we should stop asking, "Where is God?" and instead ask, "God, what do you want us, your people, to do about it? Where do you want us, your church, to go? Show us where to go and what to do, so that the world will know that you are a God who breaks chains, who loves, who is with those who suffer."

Followers of Jesus have an invitation from God to spend our lives on behalf of others—to lament for them and with them, to stand in the gap for them. We are meant to move beyond ourselves and join in a Protest lament with and for others.

The Jewish faith has a tradition of lament known as Tisha B'Av. It is the saddest day of the calendar year, a day to remember the atrocities born by the Jewish people, including the Holocaust. On Tisha B'Av, traditionally, people do not even greet one another. It's a day set aside to fast, to grieve, and to chant words from the book of Lamentations.[1]

We have much to learn from our Jewish brothers and sisters, for whom lament is an aspect of faith, not something separate from it. What if our Christian communities began to intentionally lament every illness, every destroyed family, every abuse, every communal sin, every untimely death, every loss, every heartache?

What if more churches began to communally lament the historic, violent oppression of our black brothers and sisters in this country? What if we lamented the way we've ignored indigenous peoples and other people groups? The way women have been treated for centuries? What if we lamented every hate group that acted sadistically toward the LGBTQ community and others "in the name of Jesus"?

What if we created regular space to lament the plight of war-ravaged refugees and modern-day slaves? Every school shooting? What if we lamented every aborted unborn child, while also walking closely and lovingly with women who've felt the shame of abortion? What if we began to lament, communally, in the wake of national disasters?

I'm not talking about standing with any certain political party—that can be so divisive. What I mean is this: No matter where you stand politically or theologically, we can all humble ourselves to the point of lamenting with others. In fact, lament is crucial if we want to build relational bridges with the gospel—if we want to authentically display and declare God's love to a hurting world.

I can't help but wonder—what if lament became a consistent part of the evangelical church calendar and evangelical communities? What if our response to pain became as much a part of our regular disciplines as prayer, tithing, Bible study, small groups, and other aspects of spiritual formation? I wonder if many who've been ignored or hurt by the church would come home. I wonder if our own suffering would not be quite so unbearably lonely.

Jeremiah's Model

Let's take a look at Jeremiah's lament again. Throughout Lamentations, the prophet never laments selfishly. Yes, he laments personally; he laments his own grief. But Jeremiah's lament emerges on behalf of the pain of others. He enters their pain, validates it, carries it to God. Jeremiah becomes what Michael Card calls an "intercessor of lament."[2]

Jeremiah gives in to the full force of his grief for the city he loves dearly. As he laments for Jerusalem, he reveals his intense devotion to these people. Take a look at a few verses from chapters 4 and 5:

How the precious children of Zion, once worth their
weight in gold, are now considered as pots of clay,
the work of a potter's hands!

LAMENTATIONS 4:2

Those who once ate delicacies are destitute in the
streets. Those brought up in royal purple now lie on
ash heaps.

LAMENTATIONS 4:5

The LORD has given full vent to his wrath; he has
poured out his fierce anger. He kindled a fire in Zion
that consumed her foundations.

LAMENTATIONS 4:11

Our inheritance has been turned over to strangers,
our homes to foreigners. We have become fatherless,
our mothers are widows.

LAMENTATIONS 5:2-3

Women have been violated in Zion, and virgins
in the towns of Judah.

LAMENTATIONS 5:11

The elders are gone from the city gate; the young
men have stopped their music. Joy is gone from
our hearts; our dancing has turned to
mourning.

LAMENTATIONS 5:14-15

As Jeremiah declares the woeful state of this people, he pleads with God, "Remember, LORD, what has happened to us; look, and see our disgrace" (Lamentations 5:1).

In other words: "God, you've abandoned us. You've forgotten us. You've poured out your wrath on us."

While the Lord is certainly not Israel's enemy, for this awful moment, he certainly looks like one, even feels like one. Jeremiah unashamedly expresses that sentiment on behalf of his neighbors.

This is one of the many reasons why I love Jeremiah. He says it all, unedited, unafraid. But there's something else I admire. Though he knew that the Israelites had a long history of rebellion against God, though he knew their sin was part of the reason they suffered, though they treated him horribly as he tried to intercede for them, Jeremiah can't help but feel what his people feel—devastated, angry, and broken. He can't help but love them by lamenting for them and with them.

As a prophet, Jeremiah could have easily kept his distance from the city's pain, having initially warned Jerusalem of her impending doom. He could have declared a big, fat, arrogant "I told you so." Instead, he's pastoral, a shepherd. Jeremiah becomes a fellow mourner. He enters in. "Jeremiah directly speaks God's truth, but just as important," writes Soong-Chan Rah, "Jeremiah's expression of compassion reflects God's compassion. Jeremiah's heart was broken by the things that break the heart of God."[3]

Jeremiah gives voice to the voiceless victims, to the cries of hungry children, abused mothers, and grieving fathers. He advocates for them passionately in the court of God. His example is an important model for the church today. There are a lot of times we're tempted to blame victims. We might see someone in a difficult situation and believe we know exactly what mistakes or bad life choices landed them there. We think we understand precisely what will get them out.

But even in the rare instance that we've accurately assessed someone else's circumstance, being unwilling to have compassion for them—simply because we think they deserve their situation—means we've grown arrogant enough to forget what Jesus has done for us.

In our own sin and idolatry, God showed us undeserved, abundant compassion. God has withheld nothing from us. If we can't show others the same compassion that Jeremiah showed Jerusalem—the same compassion that God, in Jesus, showed us—then we have to ask ourselves if we've grown cold to the gospel.

We know we truly love someone when we are willing to take on their pain as our own. "The degree to which I am willing to enter into the suffering of another person reveals the level of my commitment and love for them," writes musician and author Michael Card. "If I am not interested in your hurts, I am not really interested in you. Neither am I willing to suffer *to know* you nor to be known by you."[4]

This is why the demonstration of the cross is such a powerful love lament. God entered the world's suffering. He took it on his back. Lament became flesh in Jesus. It's no wonder that Jesus was mistaken for prophets like Jeremiah (Matthew 16:14).

Jeremiah's laments, like Jesus' laments, are passionate, poetic intercessory prayers of love. In this way, lament creates room at the table for all of the world's suffering. It doesn't remain blind to it. It isn't threatened by it. Lament doesn't say, "Oh, that's too political for me. I can't go there." No—biblical, godly lament gets its hands dirty. Lament mourns with *and* on behalf of the lost, the least, and the lonely.

What if, from the depths of our own struggle, we opened our eyes to the world's pain—and began to create room for their laments? What if, like Jeremiah and like Jesus, our laments led us to advocate for and truly love others?

If you and I are going to learn what it is to lament as God's people, we cannot stop at our own private laments over our own personal reality. We must ask God to give us his compassion so that we are willing to enter into the pain of our brothers and sisters.

At the end of the day, the gospel of Jesus transforms our identity and self-worth. The gospel gives us dignity, vocation, and value. The gospel impacts our personal lives and heals our identities. The gospel sets us free from shame and from the prison of our past. The gospel makes us friends with God. I will proclaim that joyfully until I die. And yet, the gospel isn't meant to stay private. The gospel is not primarily a self-help manual.

The gospel calls us—the people of God—to love him with all of our hearts, souls, minds, and strength, *and* to love our neighbors as we love ourselves. One powerful way we can show God's love to others is through our lament.

In fact, to lament with and on behalf of others is one of the high callings of the church. "The church is the Body of Christ," writes community developer and minister John Perkins. "It is to literally be the replacement of Jesus in a given community, doing what he would do, going where he would go, teaching what he would teach."[5]

Our efforts matter. Our prayers matter. Our encouraging notes matter. Our meal trains matter. Our driving a working mom's children to sports practices matters. Our helping run errands matters. Our hospitality matters. Our mowing the neighbor's lawn matters. Our hospital and prison visits matter. Our advocacy matters. Our rescue-work matters. Our helping decorate a sick person's home for Christmas matters. Our texting during the bad breakup matters. Our writing the House and the Senate matters. Our declaring the gospel in both word *and* deed matters. Our extravagant, Christ-centered love, lavishly given to the lost, the least of these, and the last matters. Our crying out with others matters.

All of it matters—all of the little ways we pour ourselves out—because we are saying, "We stand with you." We are declaring, "You are not alone"—which is, let's be honest, one of the most healing things we can say to anyone. It is a beautiful picture of the lament love of Christ and his body, the church.

———◆———

To lament is to love others. This is the missing piece for me, I realize. I've got to get out of my head, get over my Farrah Fawcett hands, and get my Protest lament on. I add another ekah to my journal: *How selfish I've been, God. Help me change. Teach me to lament with and for others.*

Here's what I eventually feel led to do. I start small, with what's right in front of me—our church plant and our neighborhood. With help from our church, Kevin and I begin to host block parties in order to build better relationships with our neighbors—so that we can actually learn their laments and know how to walk beside them.

We begin to build relationships with and learn the stories of the DREAMers in our largely Hispanic community. We lament with them, for their pain, for the abuses they have suffered, and for their fears. We stand beside them vocally, emotionally, and financially, and before our state representatives.

We host "Dinner, Documentary, and Discussion" nights at church. We invite the entire city over to share a meal and watch a movie about some issue around injustice, and then we host a time of listening, learning, and communal lament. We launch a Be the Bridge group[6] focused on racial reconciliation.

I attend nights of lament at another local church, where we sing, pray, and ask God's forgiveness for our racism, materialism, violence, and other forms of idolatry. I read more and more books by diverse authors in order to hear their narratives, in order to learn. Kevin and I meet with other Chicago church planters who are doing the real labor of loving our city. They humble me and help me to lament my own blissful naiveté.

It's not enough, I know. I'm still privileged. I have so much to learn, so much repentance to do. However, it's a beginning. I am learning to move out of my private pain into the particular pain of my incredible city.

Philippians chapter 1 says that we have the privilege not only of believing in Christ but also of suffering for him.[7] But let's get real for a minute. My suffering, as painful as it is, is not the same as suffering *for* Christ. My trials are nothing compared to the suffering of the marginalized or victimized, the suffering of sacrificial missionaries, of frontline grassroots workers, and of the persecuted church. These people are the real risk-takers, the faithful Jesus followers, the ones actually suffering for Jesus. They fight evil on a daily basis and risk their lives to live for and promote the gospel.

Yes, we need to honor our own pain. But in order to act like the people of God we're meant to be, we have to look outside of ourselves and ask El Roi to help us sincerely see the world's suffering—and do something about it. As for me, I've ignored the laments of my city and of the world for far too long. I've allowed my neighbors to lament without me. It's been my loss, and mine alone. Thankfully, God keeps expanding my understanding of his Kingdom and keeps leading me to a place where I want to honor and learn from the suffering voices of others. I know that no one needs *me* to rescue them. God is the rescuer. And yet I can't deny that God calls his people, the church, to partner with him. So I will sit with you in your pain and together we will cry out to God—because he is our only hope; he is our only way through this.

In the 2018 documentary about Mr. Rogers, *Won't You Be My Neighbor?*, Fred Rogers says something startlingly profound: "The greatest thing we can do is to help somebody know that they're loved and capable of loving."[8] This is what Protest lament does. Even though it is full of righteous anger, at its core, Protest lament is a call to love thy neighbor—a call to see the imago Dei (image of God) and the inherent value in all people.

Your Lament for Others

This morning, I look over Proverbs, once again rereading the verses that God (so sweetly) led me to all those years ago: "When you lie down, you will not be afraid; when you lie down, your sleep will be sweet. Have no fear of sudden disaster or of the ruin that overtakes the wicked, for the LORD will be at your side and will keep your foot from being snared" (Proverbs 3:24-26).

For the first time ever, this very morning, my eyes fall to the verses that follow: "Do not withhold good from those to whom it is due, when it is in your power to act. Do not say to your neighbor, 'Come back tomorrow and I'll give it to you'—when you already have it with you" (Proverbs 3:27-28).

It is in your power to act on behalf of your neighbor. I cannot believe I've never noticed these words before, about doing good to our neighbors. I sit here stupefied. I can't believe I'm seeing these verses, of all times, right now.

Is this a coincidence? Or is it possible—did God know—when he first gave me those verses nearly twenty-five years ago, that all things would come full circle? Maybe I'm over-thinking this. But did God know that while writing this very chapter about lamenting for others, I'd return to those same comforting words? Did God know—twenty-five years ago—that the following verses would be precisely what I would need right now? Has God planned this since the dawn of time? Does God, our Time Traveler, attend to our past, present, and future laments—before we even know we'll need him to?

Okay, I know the gospel isn't exclusively about me, but this very second, I'm stunned. God's love is so personal, so excessive, so showy. His Word *back then* is ministering to my heart *right now*.

In our laments, we demand God to Look! Look! Look! Believe it or not, he does. He sees. He answers. He provides. He leads. He guides. He transforms. He moves us out of our fears, out of our wills, into his—where he leads us to Look! Look! Look! at the pain of the world around us.

Desmond Tutu, the South African archbishop who tirelessly led the way in breaking down the old apartheid system, wrote this in his book *Made for Goodness*: "There are gifts hidden in suffering that can be redeemed only in the experience. . . . Compassion, which literally means 'suffering with,' may feel like the most futile kind of suffering. It changes nothing. It holds no hope of changing anything. Yet to be compassionate is to see with a God's-eye view."[9]

Your lamenting for others may look different from mine because the needs of your neighbors and your neighborhood or town may look different. The systematic injustices in your community may look different. The global laments God places on your heart may look different. That's okay.

Just ask God what he wants you to do. How does he want you to pray (Romans 8:26-27)? For whom does he want you to lament? Whose stories does God want you to learn from? Where might your laments lead to humble action on behalf of others? Where does he want you to grow in compassion? How does he want your church, his body in your community, to rise up?

No matter where you live or where you come from, it is

within your power to love your neighbor. As you lament, you reveal the compassionate hope of Jesus to a world in need. Don't rush to fix. Just listen. Learn. Be present. Bear witness. Humbly acknowledge any biases and privilege you might have.

Above all, love others as you lament with and for them. Gather with the people of God in your community and host nights of intercessory lamenting for your city and for the world. *Suffer with* and *see with a God's-eye view.*

A Lament by David, and Again by Jesus,
as He Poured Himself Out on the Cross

My God, my God, why have you forsaken me?
    Why are you so far from saving me,
    so far from my cries of anguish?
My God, I cry out by day, but you do not answer,
    by night, but I find no rest.

Yet you are enthroned as the Holy One;
    you are the one Israel praises.
In you our ancestors put their trust;
    they trusted and you delivered them.
To you they cried out and were saved;
    in you they trusted and were not put to shame.

But I am a worm and not a man,
    scorned by everyone, despised by the people.
All who see me mock me;

they hurl insults, shaking their heads.
"He trusts in the LORD," they say,
   "let the LORD rescue him.
Let him deliver him,
   since he delights in him."

Yet you brought me out of the womb;
   you made me trust in you, even at my mother's breast.
From birth I was cast on you;
   from my mother's womb you have been my God.

Do not be far from me,
   for trouble is near
   and there is no one to help. . . .

But you, LORD, do not be far from me.
   You are my strength; come quickly to help me.

PSALM 22:1-11, 19

11

what kind of God do we have?

Withness Remains

IN 2005, A DECADE BEFORE this difficult season of ours begins, Kevin convinces me to pack up what little we own into two huge duffel bags and move to Zambia, Africa. Kevin wants us to learn from and serve with his mentor and personal hero—a joyful, shalom-seeking Zambian pastor.

Kevin and I spend the year in a compound community called Mapalo, which, in the language of the Bemba tribe, means *blessing*.[1] Despite the hopeful name, it's estimated that 16.5 percent of Zambia's population is HIV positive. The life expectancy is around age forty.[2] Hunger is the norm. Waterborne diseases run rampant. Medicine men continue to practice and promote evil, sexually violent acts against women and children.

Still, somehow Bemba Christians sing a worship song: "*Mama, yo, yo, yo, ba Lesa ba weme.*" Roughly translated into English? "It blows my mind how good God is."[3]

Some people, when faced with suffering, overcome. They sing a louder song. For others, like me, it takes a while.

I wonder, as I think about my Zambian friends, how your heart is holding up these days. How's your pain? How does your lament song sound right now?

A dear friend recently asked me how to lament. Her father just died. There's been a recent rift in her family. Her sister is severely mentally ill. "I don't understand how to do this, Aubrey," she said.

I told her about ekahs and vavs. I told her about Shalom laments, Exodus laments, Protest laments, and Repentant laments. I pointed her to Hannah and Jeremiah and some other biblical examples of lamenters. I mentioned the work of *not* faking or escaping and of lamenting with others. "I don't know everything," I said. "But here is what I do know: Lament takes time. Most of all, it takes perspective. Sometimes we can't lament immediately. We don't always lament in the initial moments of our struggle. Sometimes it takes effort and repetition to strengthen our lament muscles. It takes community and grieving with others. We have to work hard at formally expressing our grief to God. We have to ask the Holy Spirit for help to lament. But whenever you begin lamenting, I have no doubt God will meet you and show you his love."

If, like my friend, you still feel lost as to how to lament, don't worry. My hope and prayer is that even if you don't know everything yet, you will begin to lean into the words of the biblical lamenters. Read through the laments I've placed throughout this book, or study your Bible for other laments. Pray those holy words aloud, back to God. Familiarize your heart with the scriptural laments, and allow God's Word to speak for you. Listen to some lament music and sing those songs to God. Ask the Holy Spirit to lament through you. Most of all, take heart—there is an end to all laments.

The End of All Laments

Another friend of mine, my college roommate who loves Jesus and knows the journey I've been on, returns from a trip to Israel with a gift for me—a photo from the garden of Gethsemane, where Jesus began his long and painful lament. The photo contains an image of a plaque that sits in the garden today. The plaque contains Jesus' own cry of the soul from Matthew 26: "My Father, if it be possible, let this cup pass from me: nevertheless not as I will, but as thou wilt."[4]

There is another quote underneath, from a writer simply known as MB: "O Jesus, in deepest night and agony You spoke these words of trust and surrender to God the Father in Gethsemane. In love and gratitude, I want to say in times of fear and distress, 'My Father, I do not understand You, but I trust You.'"

It's taken me many years and quite a long journey for my stubborn heart to say those same words—along with my Savior and others who've gone before me: *Father, I don't understand you. But I trust you. I trust that you're with me.*

The final book of Jeremiah's own song embodies this

same concept—the very essence of lament: radical acceptance. Both Jeremiah and the city of Jerusalem are drained
of striving. Both are exhausted from trying to control God's
hand. Lamentations 5 is a relinquishment of control, an
acceptance. "I give up," Jeremiah seems to say.

The final verse of Lamentations is the opposite of a trium-
phant ending. The book ends with a couple of questions and
a prayer: "Why do you always forget us? Why do you forsake
us so long? Restore us to yourself, Lord, that we may return;
renew our days as of old unless you have utterly rejected us
and are angry with us beyond measure" (5:20-22).

It may seem depressing, but Jeremiah simply states the
truth of all laments: This is horrible *and* God is trustworthy.
It's up to him if he will restore us. It's God's call if he'll rescue
us from what we're facing.

The panic of the earlier chapters is gone. Jeremiah
no longer begs God to "Look! Look! Look!" Instead, in
Lamentations 5, he humbly crumbles and accepts the reality
of suffering. *Not my will, God, but yours.*

Although Jeremiah's resignation may seem like despair,
the difference between lament and despair is a thin line—and
that line matters. Despair gives up. The word *despair* is from
the Latin *de* (down from) and *sperare* (hope).[5] Despair moves
down from hope.

Lament is the opposite. Lament moves us up to hope.

Here's the hope of all laments: Generations after the
events of Lamentations, Jesus left the comfort of heaven and
entered Jerusalem's long years of suffering. He willingly, vol-
untarily became both the object and subject of lament. In
taking upon himself the consequences for all of our sin, the

penalty for the world's idolatry, the power of death—and in taking on the principalities and forces of darkness—Jesus didn't hesitate to expose himself to the worst any person could face. Instead, he willingly bore the full weight of it all on the cross. After years of longing, after generations of lament—through the suffering of their very own King—the Israelites were, as we are, healed.

Because of the Cross and the Kingdom—because of the sin-atoning, penalty-paying, God-and-humanity-reconciling, death-defying, bondage-breaking, heart-healing, prisoner-emancipating, forgiveness-bringing, adoption-declaring, heaven-and-earth-meeting, new-creation-ushering, shalom-restoring, victory-winning, evil-overcoming, righteousness-gifting, Spirit-filling work of the Cross and the Resurrection—pain and suffering will *never* be the end of our story. All laments—from Job's to Jeremiah's, from Hannah's to yours—are answered in the lament-ending love of Jesus. Lament is the up-to-hope journey because it is ultimately the up-to-Jesus journey.

Our hope in suffering is never found by striving to see the positive or looking on the bright side. Hope for the Christian is always about the *object* of our hope, the one all laments long for and lead to, the embodiment and answer of all laments: Jesus. By his suffering, we are saved in ours.

What kind of God do we have? This seems to be the central question of all laments. Is this a God who sits in some distant location, far removed, arbitrarily choosing to keep his people in the dark while they suffer? Is this a God who hides his presence or his purposes from his people in order to make them live out some cosmic guessing game?[6]

Lament declares that we have a God who hears, a God who speaks, a God who sees, a God who opens our eyes to see him, a God who calls us by name, a God who invites us into his purposes for the world. Even when we are wandering and doubting—even when we are far from where we should be, even when we are facing the worst—God is close.

What kind of God do we have? He is not a passive, distant, deistic God, but an incarnate God. A God who reveals his *withness* in our darkest hours. An Immanuel God, a God who is transcendent over all creation but immanent with his people.

Lament helps us join in that ancient song about our God—*I am my beloved's and he is mine, and his banner over me is love* (Song of Songs 6:3; 2:4). We may not understand this pain, but we can trust his plan, his power, and his presence.

God and Evil

As time goes on, and as we inevitably face new kinds of trials, we will likely continue to ask that question—*What kind of God do we have?* In our journeys to find the answer, we might rub up against the topic of *theodicy*. Taken from two words, *theòs* (God) and *díkē* (justice), theodicy is an attempt to answer the BIG WHY—the ontological problem of the existence of evil and God's justice.[7] How could a purportedly good God allow evil to exist?

The difficulty with theodicy is that there are just no easy or quick answers for real pain, suffering, spiritual attack, or evil. That said, in considering some of these things myself over the years, I wanted to share some theodical thoughts that have given me courage. I hope they encourage you as well.

- *God is not the creator of evil and suffering. He is the creator of very good.* As pastor and author Lee Strobel says, "This answers the question you hear so often: 'Why didn't God merely create a world where tragedy and suffering didn't exist?' The answer is, He did!"[8] Genesis reminds us that, although we were never promised an uncomplicated world, everything God created was originally good.

- *Where did suffering come from?* Let's call it what it is: idolatry. Our sin, selfishness, inaction, apathy, and hatred have brought pain into this world. As Romans 5:12 says, "Just as sin entered the world through one man, and death through sin, . . . in this way death came to all people, because all sinned." But now, you might think of an important follow-up question:

- *What of tragedies or suffering we didn't cause?* For these instances, perhaps we need to embrace a broader definition of sin. Because sin is not just "doing bad things"; sin impacts the globe. Sin kills innocent victims. Illness, natural disasters, corrupt and evil leaders, abusive parents, starving children: Sin's impact reaches far—not only affecting our personal lives but also the entire planet, the world's health, and our relationships with God and with each other. This is what makes the gospel so powerful: The Cross destroys the stronghold of sin—not just personally, but also cosmically—and will one day make all things right for those who call upon the name of the Lord.

- *We have a spiritual enemy, but more powerfully still, we have the tools to fight back.* God did not bring evil into the world, or into our lives, but principalities of darkness exist. Ephesians 6:12 reminds us that "our struggle is not against flesh and blood, but against the rulers, against the authorities, against the powers of this dark world and against the spiritual forces of evil in the heavenly realms." Even if we don't have all the answers now about the existence of evil or spiritual attack, what we *do* have is God's Spirit, God's Word, God's righteousness, God's truth, God's salvation, God's shalom, God's justice, God's resurrection power, God's presence, and the armor of God. We don't fight our spiritual enemy alone. We fight under the banner of the King of kings, who has already claimed the victory.

- *God doesn't always prevent suffering, but he always transforms it.* Ecclesiastes tells us that God makes all things beautiful in his time (3:11). James tells us that we can count all of our trials and struggles as joy, because our pain produces faithful perseverance and maturity (1:2-4). Genesis tells us that God takes the very things that evil intends to use to destroy us and turns them into good (50:20). Hebrews reminds us that since we are flesh and blood, he became flesh and blood, "so that by his death he might break the power of him who holds the power of death—that is, the devil—and free those who all their lives were held in slavery by their fear of death" (2:14-15). In his penultimate act of transformation, by Jesus' death and suffering, God destroyed the power of death and suffering. But let's never forget the lengths Jesus went to for our rescue, and the depths from which he has ransomed those who repent and follow Jesus. He has moved us from death to life. The gospel is such massive, good news.

• *Jesus heals people.* James says, "Is anyone among you in trouble? Let them pray. Is anyone happy? Let them sing songs of praise. Is anyone among you sick? Let them call the elders of the church to pray over them and anoint them with oil in the name of the Lord. And the prayer offered in faith will make the sick person well; the Lord will raise them up. If they have sinned, they will be forgiven. Therefore confess your sins to each other and pray for each other so that you may be healed. The prayer of a righteous person is powerful and effective."[9]

Though God does not heal everyone immediately, we know from Scripture and from modern-day stories that communities of Christians all over the globe experience God's profound healing every day. And Jesus uses the church, his body, as a tool for alleviating the suffering of others. In Jesus, there is healing for emotional, spiritual, and physical suffering. We are not stuck in our suffering forever. Jesus will heal now on earth and fully in the new creation.

• *God has the final word.* One day, suffering will cease. Evil will be shut down forever. We will see his new creation. We will see heaven meeting earth. We long to see it now, but 2 Peter 3:9 tells us that God is patiently waiting, not wanting anyone to perish but wanting everyone to come to repentance. God's love and compassion are the delay, not his apathy or ineffectiveness. In Revelation 21:5, Jesus himself declares from his throne, "I am making everything new!"

In our suffering, and in life's inexplicable mysteries, we can take courage. We may never be able to answer all of the hard questions. But think about it—the very fact that the evil in our world feels wrong and unjust, that sense we have that life should restore, uplift, and renew—that itself is the grace of God at work in us, revealing that *more* beyond our laments is on the way.

From Bitter to Blessing

Mapalo, our beloved African city, is also revealing that *more* is on the way. Mapalo wasn't always called *blessing*. Its original name, Chipilukusu, means deformed or structureless.[10] Our Zambian friends once told us it also means bitter, broken, or cursed. But Zambian Christians, determined to be labeled by something other than suffering, petitioned their local government to change their name.

Today, as you walk into this compound community, you can see a sign where *Chipilukusu* has been crossed out. Spray-painted over it in dynamic lettering is *Mapalo*. Blessing on top of brokenness.

What kind of God do we have? I see him so clearly in the people of Mapalo. After changing their city's name, the Mapalo Christians built a church and a medical clinic. They established a school and developed a clean-water initiative. They found a way to bring in electricity and began to turn on lights for their people. They educated women and men about the realities of HIV. They began to speak against witch doctors' evil practices that promote and spread diseases. And they built a smooth dirt road through the compound so that the entire community has easy and permanent access to it all. They have brought the Kingdom of God to their city.

It's not that starvation, sickness, or sexual violence has been eradicated. It's that the Bemba Christians have spent many long, hard years in lament, and in lamenting as a city, they have created a pathway from pain to possibility, from their *hows* to their *yets* to their *withs*.

I long to follow in their example—even as in my own lament journey, something new has now begun: another expression of illness. My hands and arms, up to the elbows, have started to go numb. I call them my "dead fish arms." I'm getting EMGs and cortisone shots and occupational therapy, but something is not adding up. There will always be mystery in lament, I suppose. *Yet* I remember that most laments follow the Exodus journey—and I remember an important moment from the Exodus.

Just after God rescues his people from the Red Sea, they once again complain and cry out. In the midst of their lament, Moses says this, "The LORD will fight for you; you need only to be still" (Exodus 14:14).

It's as though God is singing a lullaby over the Israelites, inviting them into rest. *Shhh. Hush now. I've got you. Quiet*

*your soul. Silence your lament. Get some sleep, little ones. You
are invited to be still now and know that I am God.*

So I will accept that invitation, this invitation.

Just as I pray you accept yours.

"The God of all grace," wrote St. Peter, "who called you
to his eternal glory in Christ, after you have suffered a little
while, will himself restore you and make you strong, firm and
steadfast" (1 Peter 5:10).

This is the hope. This is why we lament. Because we
believe that one day all things will be made new. One day,
Jesus will end suffering forever.

When all feels lost, take courage, friend. God's *withness*
remains.

> *A Lament*
>
> God—
>
> **How** have we come to this? You and I, who used
>   to be so close, so connected.
>
> Are you near?
>
> Loneliness, unseenness surround me. And my
>   hips, oh God, my knees, my ankles, my toes,
>   my hands, my neck, my fingers all embody
>   my sadness—they ache with sadness and
>   misery.
>
> I don't want to think of you as a withholding Father
>   but I have thought of you that way.
>
> I'm asking you, God, for healing, but it feels like
>   you are ignoring me. Where are you?

Are you even real? Are you a figment of my
      imagination, or a construct?
I'm panicking that I'll never hear from you again.
Yet I remember how you have carried me in the past.
I remember, God, all the ways that you have
      stepped in to show me you are real.
I remember how you have cared for my family,
      my loved ones, my community.
I know, Jesus, your rugged cross and
      your resurrection power.
Please take my confusion, doubt, grief, and
      suffering in your capable hands.
Place them near your heart; care for them,
      transform them—and me—while you're at it.
Redeem this pain somehow.
God, you are judge and King.
God, you are comfort.
God, you are peace.
God, you are love.
Without your hand pulling me up,
I will never be able to move from my mourning bench.
But **with** your hand at my side, I will make a joyful
      noise unto the Lord.
Jesus, you are my strength, my salvation,
      and my louder song.

APPENDIX A

advice

(or not)

AT A WOMEN'S RETREAT, I open up for the first time about my illness. I talk about how I feel ashamed of it, how it redefines me. I speak about how I used to run and exercise but how I can't do much of that anymore, at least not in the same way. I tell these ladies that I know this disease didn't attack the brain, but sometimes my brain just wants a break from having to process this new reality.

I don't say this at the retreat, but I actually begin to feel grateful for pain's unique counsel. I start to believe that life's pains can surprisingly become gifts. Suffering shakes up everything, but eventually, it all must settle. With Jesus at our side, it all settles on hope.

A woman walks up to me after I finish speaking. She wears amber-colored bracelets on one arm, stacked all the way up to her elbow. "Can I offer you some advice?" she asks.

At this point in my illness, I receive a lot of unsolicited advice, and I've grown a little cynical. I confess that my thoughts are not full of gratitude. I think, *Oh, great, here we go again. Let me guess. Is it turmeric? Is it Paleo? Is it the magical bracelets you're wearing?*

She continues, "When you feel like crap, order takeout. Don't cook and don't you dare feel guilty about it. If you can't show up, don't. If you need to take time off, take it. If you want to wear a hat because your hair is falling out, spend some money on a great hat. If you want to eat chocolate, keep chocolate stocked in the pantry. And if you can't run because you experience too much pain, don't run. Rest. Because, my dear, you have value; you are worthy of self-care."

I compliment her bracelets and tell her it's the best advice I've ever received.

If you've ever been in a hard season, you know that advice is a tricky thing. It's well meant, of course. But in their attempt to be helpful, a lot of people can say stuff that's, well . . . not. So if you're walking with someone who's going through some serious pain, here's are some genuine ways you can help without giving advice.

- Know that the grieving person will always be a grieving person—from now on. They know this, but sometimes we need to accept it, and sometimes we need to become less awkard about and around our loved one's grief. Their grief might become less raw over the years. But grief remains with a person his or her whole life. God will use grief to shape them, and draw them closer to himself. You cannot fix or take away their pain. But you can sit beside them as they cry or listen while they talk about their loss. You can allow them to scream and fall down crying and say unedited things without correcting them.

- Grieving people are afraid that you will either forget their pain or forget the one they've lost. It helps if you remember anniversaries of deaths or birthdays or diagnoses. Send cards or a text on those days. Share memories you have of their loved ones. Remind them that you see them.

- The person in pain doesn't need you to help steer them to the bright side. In fact, they might need the opposite—validation. Assure them that what they are going through is a big deal—and can be a big deal for as long as they need it to be.

- Err on the side of coming near. Err on the side of being made a fool. Err on the side of saying *I'm sorry* more than you should, even if you had nothing to do with their sorrow. Err on the side of letting your wife or husband or sister or friend grieve longer than you think he or she should. Be intentional to embrace their grief without fear. Ask open-ended questions: *How is your grief today? How is your heart? What are you thinking about?* And listen. Sometimes the grieving person needs space. But mostly they want to be met where they grieve. Practice the ministry of presence. This is, after all, what the hurting person wants—friends who are near, who minimize nothing, who lament with.

- For people in chronic pain, it can feel like an imposition to ask for help. But they need help. Here are some practical things to offer:

  > "I made dinner/grabbed a latte for you. It's on your front porch."

  > "I rented every version of *Pride and Prejudice*. Can I bring them over one night? You can pick your favorite Mr. Darcy. PS: It's always Colin Firth."

  > "I rented every Marvel movie for you. You can pick your favorite Avenger. PS: It's always Thor."

  > "Can I come over and pray for you/with you? I won't linger."

  > "Choose one of the following and I will do it for you today: (a) take your kids away from you for a couple of hours; (b) do your laundry at my house; or (c) take you for a night out."

  > "I paid for a housecleaner to come to your house this week."

You get the idea. Generally speaking, practical help and lots of compassion are all you need to offer. (And yes, it's not lost on me that this is an advice list about not giving advice. I like to think of myself not as a hypocrite but as meta.)

APPENDIX B

verses to
cling to
in pain

IN THIS SECTION ARE a few Bible verses that have meant a lot to me in this season. I don't generally love the idea of pulling verses out of context. But sometimes when we are hurting, we just need some easy-access encouragement. For the days you come to life's table feeling empty instead of full, may you find strength in God's Word.

Consider turning these verses into prayers or words of praise, adapting the "What This Says about God" section for each topic: "God, I praise you, because you are . . ."

Encouragement for Brokenheartedness	
Scripture	"He heals the brokenhearted and binds up their wounds. He determines the number of the stars and calls them each by name. Great is our Lord and mighty in power; his understanding has no limit." PSALM 147:3-5
What This Says about God	God is caring, healing, great, mighty, powerful, all-knowing, and limitless.
What This Says about You	He stands right by your side, making you whole, bringing you his healing. He understands everything you face. You are not alone. The God who named each star—whose power is unending—is with you and in you.
Encouragement for Fear	
Scripture	"Be strong and courageous. Do not be afraid or terrified because of them, for the LORD your God goes with you; he will never leave you nor forsake you." DEUTERONOMY 31:6
What This Says about God	God is an "alongsider." He never abandons or rejects his children. He is a good Father.
What This Says about You	You can be strong and have courage. You are not imprisoned by fear because God is here, right now, setting you free.

Encouragement *for* **Discouragement**

Scripture	"What, then, shall we say in response to this? If God is for us, who can be against us? He who did not spare his own Son, but gave him up for us all—how will he not also, along with him, graciously give us all things? Who will bring any charge against those whom God has chosen? It is God who justifies. Who then is the one who condemns? No one. Christ Jesus who died—more than that, who was raised to life—is at the right hand of God and is also interceding for us." ROMANS 8:31-34
What This Says about God	God is on his children's side. He is generous, extravagant in his love. He is the judge of all. He is gracious, giving, and self-sacrificing. He is a prayer warrior, praying on our behalf. He never condemns those who follow him.
What This Says about You	God is *for* you. Jesus loves you so much that he gave his own life for you. That would have been enough, but he also gives you gifts—his presence, his blessings, even his prayers. He doesn't condemn you but forgives you, shapes you, and justifies you. Jesus talks to God about you, about your needs and your heart.

Encouragement *for* **Grief**

Scripture	"Very truly I tell you, you will weep and mourn while the world rejoices. You will grieve, but your grief will turn to joy. A woman giving birth to a child has pain because her time has come; but when her baby is born she forgets the anguish because of her joy that a child is born into the world. So with you: Now is your time of grief, but I will see you again and you will rejoice, and no one will take away your joy." JOHN 16:20-22
What This Says about God	He is a joy-giver and the author of joy. His joy is permanent and indestructible and can't be taken away. He transforms pain and labor into delight.
What This Says about You	This sadness and grief will not have the final word in your life. God will one day turn it all into joy.

Encouragement *for* **Loneliness**

Scripture	"Have I not commanded you? Be strong and courageous. Do not be afraid; do not be discouraged, for the LORD your God will be with you wherever you go." JOSHUA 1:9
What This Says about God	He is strong, dependable, and enduring. He is worthy of praise and glory. He calls and restores.
What This Says about You	You are strong. You are courageous. You are never alone.

Encouragement for **Pain**

Scripture	"No discipline seems pleasant at the time, but painful. Later on, however, it produces a harvest of righteousness and peace for those who have been trained by it. Therefore, strengthen your feeble arms and weak knees. 'Make level paths for your feet,' so that the lame may not be disabled, but rather healed." HEBREWS 12:11-13 (I like how *THE MESSAGE* ends verse 13: "Help each other out. And run for it!")
What This Says about God	His path produces righteousness and peace, because he *is* righteousness. He is our peace.
What This Says about You	This season of difficulty is super hard. But if you continue to pursue Jesus, it will produce righteousness, peace, and strength in you. You can keep going, because God is doing something with all of this. He's using this season to shape you and those you love. You can endure.

Encouragement for **Suffering**

Scripture	"And the God of all grace, who called you to his eternal glory in Christ, after you have suffered a little while, will himself restore you and make you strong, firm and steadfast. To him be the power for ever and ever. Amen." 1 PETER 5:10-11
What This Says about God	He is strong, dependable, and enduring. He is worthy of praise and glory. He calls and restores.
What This Says about You	God calls you his own. He calls you into grace. He calls you into eternal glory with Jesus. This suffering season won't last forever. One day you will see Jesus face to face. You will experience his wholeness.

Encouragement for **Weakness**

Scripture	"But we have this treasure in jars of clay to show that this all-surpassing power is from God and not from us. We are hard pressed on every side, but not crushed; perplexed, but not in despair; persecuted, but not abandoned; struck down, but not destroyed. We always carry around in our body the death of Jesus, so that the life of Jesus may be revealed in our body." 2 CORINTHIANS 4:7-10
What This Says about God	The presence of Jesus gives us hope, no matter how horrible things are. He gives life through his death. He is a protector.
What This Says about You	You will not be consumed because the death and life of Jesus are stronger than anything you face.

Encouragement *for* **Weariness**

Scripture	"Do you not know? Have you not heard? The LORD is the everlasting God, the Creator of the ends of the earth. He will not grow tired or weary, and his understanding no one can fathom. He gives strength to the weary and increases the power of the weak. Even youths grow tired and weary, and young men stumble and fall; but those who hope in the LORD will renew their strength. They will soar on wings like eagles; they will run and not grow weary, they will walk and not be faint." ISAIAH 40:28-31
What This Says about God	God is everlasting, always awake and at work. He sees all, understands all, and never grows tired or stressed. He never "gets over it." He is so strong, so renewing. He is powerful.
What This Says about You	You have access to God's strength, endurance, and energy. His power is in you, empowering and enabling your body, mind, soul, and heart to keep going. You are not hopeless—because Jesus is your hope!

your
lament
journey

IN ORDER TO ENCOURAGE YOU in your own lament journey, I've compiled a little guide here connected to each chapter. It includes corresponding questions (in case you want to read this book with your community or a small group, which I highly recommend) and a 5 Rs study guide. As you go through these, I am praying for you—that you'll experience the fullness of God's healing presence in your game change, that you'll find a pathway through your pain.

Chapter 1

Reflection

1. What "game changes" are you or your loved ones facing right now?

2. How has this impacted your faith journey? Your relationship with Jesus?

3. Does this difficulty bring up any pain from the past? Have you experienced anything like this before? If so, when?

4. Who do you know who has modeled strength and courage in the midst of great difficulty? If you can't think of someone from your own life, perhaps think of a man or woman from the Bible or someone in history. Share an example.

5. Make a list of any fears, doubts, anger, or mixed emotions that you have about your current hard situation. Don't edit yourself. Let it all out, and ask God to reveal himself to you in this difficult season.

6. Spend some time as a group praying for one another. If you aren't in a group, spend some time praying for a friend in game change.

5 Rs

First, thank the Holy Spirit for being with you. Ask God's Spirit to guide your time, help you discern his voice, and assist you in tuning your awareness to God's presence. Then:

- **Read** Job 1 (and the entire book of Job, if you'd like). We can't talk about suffering without addressing the wisdom of Job. Job warns us to avoid reducing God's moral rule to easy, understandable formulas[1] and to be wise when seeking the counsel of others in these painful seasons.

  Job's story is not an easy one to swallow. It's difficult to understand why God allowed him to experience such grief. Here's the point: The Lord gives and the Lord removes. But all the while, our role is to keep on praising him and to stay intimately connected to him. After losing everything, Job remained a solid worshiper of God. And Job saw God bless him with twice as much as he lost.

- **React.** What are your initial thoughts about this passage? What words, images, or questions come to mind as you read? Don't judge yourself. Just notice and jot down the things that cross your mind.

- **Rehearse**, which comes from an old Anglo-French phrase meaning "to go over again, . . . to rake over, turn over."[2] Read the Scriptures again, this time aloud, and note any repeating words or phrases. Pay attention to themes. Observe what else is happening around these Scriptures. What might God be saying about himself here?

- **Receive**, asking God what he wants you to hear. Stay quiet, attentive. Listen for his still, small voice. Pay attention for an image, word, verse, or any thought that he brings to mind. Wait patiently. If you don't hear anything, that's okay. Just tell him that and keep going.

- **Respond** by writing, drawing, or creating a prayer (of lament and hope, if you'd like) based on your reading today.

Chapter 2

Reflection

1. How comfortable do you feel complaining to God?
   Are you prone to pour it all out or keep it all in? What
   helps or prevents you from being honest before him?

2. What do you think about this statement from
   chapter 2? "If we never acknowledge our pain to God,
   we will never truly know what it means to praise him
   on the other side of suffering. It is in our honest crying
   out *to God* about our pain that our worship *of God*
   grows more authentic. It is in this kind of relationship,
   this kind of honesty with God, that our walks with
   him become real. Lament is part of the rhythm of a
   deepening relationship with him."

3. Chapter 2 lists four expressions of lament. Which
   one do you connect with most, and why? What other
   expressions of lament have you come across?

4. Is there a particular person or issue about which you feel passionate? What would it look like to begin protesting to God on their behalf?

5. After reading chapter 2, how would you define lament? What is the value in lamenting to God?

5 Rs

Thank the Holy Spirit for being with you. Ask God's Spirit to guide your time, help you discern his voice, and assist you in tuning your awareness to God's presence. Then:

- **Read** Hannah's lament and the story of the birth of Samuel in 1 Samuel 1. The lament of a mother—especially regarding infertility or the loss of a child—is one of the most fragile kinds of laments we can experience. God provided a child for Hannah, but he doesn't always do so. And in Hannah's case, she immediately released him to God. "The LORD brings death and makes alive; he brings down to the grave and raises up," Hannah prays. "The LORD sends poverty and wealth; he humbles and he exalts" (1 Samuel 2:6-7). What can we learn from Hannah's wisdom?

- **React.** What are your initial thoughts about this passage? What words, images, or questions come to mind as you read? Jot down the things that cross your mind.

- **Rehearse**. Read the Scriptures again, this time aloud, and note any repeating words or phrases. Pay attention to themes. What might God be saying about himself here?

- **Receive**, asking God what he wants you to hear. Stay quiet, attentive. Listen for his still, small voice. Pay attention for an image, word, verse, or any thought that he brings to mind.

- **Respond** by writing, drawing, or creating a prayer (of lament and hope, if you'd like) based on your reading today.

Chapter 3

Reflection

1. Have you grown up learning about lament? If so, talk about its importance in your walk with God. If not, share why lament wasn't a part of your growing-up experience. What are the challenges to lamenting?

2. Have you ever wondered if God truly hears you? In your own life, how has God confirmed his presence, his existence? How have you seen him work?

3. Do you struggle to give yourself permission to lament? Do you find it difficult to give God all of your pain and grief? Why do you think that is?

4. What ekahs (translated *hows*, but feel free to throw in your *wheres*, *whys*, and *how longs*) do you want to ask of God? Make a list—unfiltered, unedited—and read your questions aloud to God. He hears you and he can handle it. You are invited into his throne room to speak openly.

5. Consider purchasing a lament journal, or creating a lament pin board on Pinterest, or starting a lament note in your phone. If you're artistically inclined, grab a lament sketch pad. In whatever way you can, begin to create a safe space to offer your laments to God.

6. If you could hear God say anything to you while you are in this season, what words would you like to hear from him? What would you like God to do? How do you want him to show up?

5 Rs

Thank the Holy Spirit for being with you. Ask God's Spirit to guide your time, help you discern his voice, and assist you in tuning your awareness to God's presence. Then:

- **Read** all of Psalm 55. This psalm of David is known as a "maskil," a teaching lament. It was written in order to educate others. David is a man who was intimately acquainted with grief, loss, death, fear, and regret. What might David's lament teach you?

- **React**. What are your initial thoughts about this passage? What words, images, or questions come to mind as you read? Jot down the things that cross your mind.

- **Rehearse**. Read the Scriptures again, this time aloud, and note any repeating words or phrases. Pay attention to themes. What might God be saying about himself here?

- **Receive**, asking God what he wants you to hear. Stay quiet, attentive. Listen for his still, small voice. Pay attention for an image, word, verse, or any thought that he brings to mind.

- **Respond** by writing, drawing, or creating a prayer (of lament and hope, if you'd like) based on your reading today.

Chapter 4

Reflection

1. The too-soon loss of a loved one is probably the most painful thing we can experience on this earth. Is there anyone you've had to say good-bye to? Spend some time talking about that person's influence on your life and how their death marked you. (I know this is a difficult topic. Only do this when you feel safe and ready.)

2. What questions/frustrations/confusions do you have for God about this loss? Take some time to honestly express your feelings to him and, if you're with a group, to them.

3. How do you keep going in grief? What/who gives you strength on the really bad days?

4. Has God surprised you with his love in this difficult season? What beauty from ashes have you experienced?

5. If you were walking with a friend in grief, what would you say to her? Ask God to write those same tender words on your own soul.

5 Rs

Thank the Holy Spirit for being with you. Ask God's Spirit to guide your time, help you discern his voice, and assist you in tuning your awareness to God's presence. Then:

- **Read** Psalm 88. This psalm, written by the sons of Korah, is perhaps one of the most hopeless in all of Scripture. And yet, the hope is that it is a song written to the Lord. It expresses the epitome of lament: Terrors surround us, and God is our only hope.

The sons of Korah came from a family line of deep sorrow and grief. After rebelling against God, their ancestors were killed dramatically, being swallowed up by the earth. But God spared these boys. They grew up to become significant worship leaders in the Tabernacle during King David's day.[3] Of all the psalms, eleven are attributed to them. (Bonus: Read their family's story in Numbers 16.)

- **React.** What are your initial thoughts about this passage? What words, images, or questions come to mind as you read? Jot down the things that cross your mind.

- **Rehearse.** Read the Scriptures again, this time aloud, and note any repeating words or phrases. Pay attention to themes. What might God be saying about himself here?

- **Receive**, asking God what he wants you to hear. Stay quiet, attentive. Listen for his still, small voice. Pay attention for an image, word, verse, or any thought that he brings to mind.

- **Respond** by writing, drawing, or creating a prayer (of lament and hope, if you'd like) based on your reading today.

Chapter 5

Reflection

1. In what ways has your pain made you angry, disappointed, or sad? In what other ways have you responded to your difficult situation?

2. What advice has been especially helpful to you? What advice would you give (or not give) to a friend in pain?

3. Pain can affect many of the things you used to love or enjoy. What has it robbed you of? Are there little ways you can begin to restore those things or bring new versions of those things into your life?

4. What *supposed to*s do you feel pressured with? What *supposed to*s can you permit yourself to release? What *supposed to*s are, on the other hand, from God?

5. Think back over the course of your life. In what ways has God made it abundantly clear that he loves you and is with you? (If this is difficult to answer, ask God for the grace to help you see his hand on your life over the years. Or ask a friend how they've witnessed God at work in your life.)

6. Pain can be a wise teacher. What has pain taught you? What has God taught you through pain?

7. Is your relationship with God different now than it was before experiencing a difficult season? If so, in what ways?

5 Rs

Thank the Holy Spirit for being with you. Ask God's Spirit to guide your time, help you discern his voice, and assist you in tuning your awareness to God's presence. Then:

- **Read** Psalm 74, a psalm of Asaph. Asaph was another worship leader in King David's court. He was appointed specifically to play music before the Ark of the Covenant. You can read about Asaph in 1 Chronicles 16. Asaph was a musician, artist, and prophetic voice. In Psalm 74, Asaph asks God to remember, while simultaneously reminding his hearers that God is the living God, the creator, ruler, and judge—and that he has the right to do as he pleases. He is also a compassionate God, bringing us the gift of salvation.

- **React**. What are your initial thoughts about this passage? What words, images, or questions come to mind as you read? Jot down the things that cross your mind.

- **Rehearse**. Read the Scriptures again, this time aloud, and note any repeating words or phrases. Pay attention to themes. What might God be saying about himself here?

- **Receive**, asking God what he wants you to hear. Stay quiet, attentive. Listen for his still, small voice. Pay attention for an image, word, verse, or any thought that he brings to mind.

- **Respond** by writing, drawing, or creating a prayer (of lament and hope, if you'd like) based on your reading today.

Chapter 6

Reflection

1. How has a season of pain impacted your relationships? What are some challenging and encouraging (negative and positive) examples?

2. Is there a relational conflict you've been hiding from or are afraid to really face? If so, can you ask God to tenderly help you reconnect to your loved ones? If some of your important relationships have been strained, can you reach out and ask someone, like a counselor, for help?

3. In difficult times we can easily forget the work of soul care—what we enjoy, what makes us feel loved and cared for. What do you delight in doing? What makes you feel loved and cared for? How can you begin to invite some of those things back into your life today?

4. Watching a child suffer is one of the most difficult tasks imaginable. If you have experienced this, take some time to share your child's story with your group or write about it in your lament journal. Share any ongoing prayer requests or needs that you have related to your child(ren). If you don't have any children, think of any young loved one in pain. Take time to lament on their behalf.

5. How can you begin investing in your most important relationships today? What can you do to strengthen those relationships?

5 Rs

Thank the Holy Spirit for being with you. Ask God's Spirit to guide your time, help you discern his voice, and assist you in tuning your awareness to God's presence. Then:

- **Read** Psalm 38. Michael Card calls this psalm "A Penitent Sufferer's Plea for Healing."[4] Essentially, David is petitioning, begging God to heal him, while asking for forgiveness because sickness, loneliness, and guilt are plaguing him. In our own seasons of illness, loneliness, and regret, this psalm is a good word of encouragement. God faithfully helps and rescues.

- **React**. What are your initial thoughts about this passage? What words, images, or questions come to mind as you read? Jot down the things that cross your mind.

- **Rehearse**. Read the Scriptures again, this time aloud, and note any repeating words or phrases. Pay attention to themes. What might God be saying about himself here?

- **Receive**, asking God what he wants you to hear. Stay quiet, attentive. Listen for his still, small voice. Pay attention for an image, word, verse, or any thought that he brings to mind.

- **Respond** by writing, drawing, or creating a prayer (of lament and hope, if you'd like) based on your reading today.

Chapter 7

Reflection

1. Do you suffer from chronic physical pain or have a friend who does? What about a long-term painful situation of some other kind? Describe your experience or your friend's experience (without divulging private information, of course). When and how did it begin? How are you/they dealing with it day by day?

2. Chapter 7 mentions "getting weird" on Facebook. In what ways do you tend to escape when wanting to avoid reality? What would it look like to stop running to those escapes?

3. Knowledge of self is a powerful way to understand how you process pain and grief and why you react the way you do. Are you stuck in a season of self-pity or comparison? If so, take some time this week asking God to help you get out of that trap.

4. *Radical acceptance* is the ability to embrace your life, no matter how hard it is. Ask God to help you radically accept yourself and this season. What are some areas in which you need his help so that pain doesn't defeat you?

5. What alternative version of the present—with its what-might-have-beens—do you need to lament and hand over to God? This might take some time to think through. Be kind, patient, and gracious with yourself as you think through and grieve these. Ask some trustworthy friends to cover you in prayer, as this can be an emotional process.

6. What words of healing and encouragement can you speak over yourself now? Not over your fantasy self or your false self, but over the real you, now? What words of healing will you say over your hurting body and soul? Take this moment to write those down or speak them aloud.

7. What have been some moments when God revealed glimpses of glory in your times of struggle?

5 Rs

Thank the Holy Spirit for being with you. Ask God's Spirit to guide your time, help you discern his voice, and assist you in tuning your awareness to God's presence. Then:

- **Read** Isaiah 54. This passage is all about glory through suffering. God's covenant relationship with his people (as expressed through Abraham[5] and with Noah[6]), leads to the ultimate covenant, God's unstoppable covenant of love through Jesus Christ. It is *his* suffering that saves us. As a result, we ourselves are saved through suffering. In times of trial, it may feel as though God has abandoned you, but we can be sure this is not so! He is forever faithful to his covenant promises—all of which are fulfilled in Jesus.

- **React.** What are your initial thoughts about this passage? What words, images, or questions come to mind as you read? Jot down the things that cross your mind.

- **Rehearse.** Read the Scriptures again, this time aloud, and note any repeating words or phrases. Pay attention to themes. What might God be saying about himself here?

- **Receive**, asking God what he wants you to hear. Stay quiet, attentive. Listen for his still, small voice. Pay attention for an image, word, verse, or any thought that he brings to mind.

- **Respond** by writing, drawing, or creating a prayer (of lament and hope, if you'd like) based on your reading today.

Chapter 8

Reflection

1. In painful situations, have you struggled to rest in God's presence? If not, what are some ways you've stayed connected with him?

2. When do you most often sense the presence of God with you?

3. Sometimes we walk through overwhelming situations and God says, "Hey, don't panic, because this difficult place is precisely where I am going to meet you and reveal myself to you. This is where you will learn the true meaning of *yet*." In what ways do you think you "needed" your hard season?

4. Are there certain attitudes you've had that you need to ask God's forgiveness for?

5. If you don't already have one, take some time this week to identify a spiritual mentor or spiritual director who can help you dive deeper into your relationship with God or help you work through any doubts you may have about God.

6. Do you feel like you're approaching a vav season? Have your ekahs begun to turn into hope? Share some ways that might be true.

5 Rs

Thank the Holy Spirit for being with you. Ask God's Spirit to guide your time, help you discern his voice, and assist you in tuning your awareness to God's presence. Then:

- **Read** Lamentations 3. Jeremiah's entire lament hinges on this chapter. He has been grieving the downfall of his people, his city, his holy Temple. Yet here, he reveals a heart of hope. Jeremiah knows that even when all hope is lost, God's *hesed*, his unfailing love, stands firm.[7]

- **React.** What are your initial thoughts about this passage? What words, images, or questions come to mind as you read? Jot down the things that cross your mind.

- **Rehearse.** Read the Scriptures again, this time aloud, and note any repeating words or phrases. Pay attention to themes. Observe what else is happening around these Scriptures. What might God be saying about himself here?

- **Receive,** asking God what he wants you to hear. Stay quiet, attentive. Listen for his still, small voice. Pay attention for an image, word, verse, or any thought that he brings to mind.

- **Respond** by writing, drawing, or creating a prayer (of lament and hope, if you'd like) based on your reading today.

Chapter 9

Reflection

1. Chapter 9 speaks of finding reassurance in Mark 4 during a difficult season. What about you? What Scriptures do you find encouraging?

2. Choose a few verses (you can find many throughout this book to get you started, including in appendix B) to serve as a beacon of hope. Record those verses on your phone or in your journal—somewhere where you will have easy access to them. Begin to pray now, privately or in your group, for God to make his words true in your soul. What verses did you choose?

3. What spiritual practices do you find most helpful as a way to reconnect with God? Are you regularly walking through them? If not, what would it look like for you to make that happen?

4. Would you be willing to begin praying, "God, if you're real, make yourself real to me"? What's one way you'd love for him to answer?

5. Think of one area in which you need to experience more of the power and authority of Jesus. Ask him to reveal his power to you.

6. Think of another area in which you need to experience more of his comforting, healing presence. Ask him to reveal a vision of his presence to you.

7. In both cases (from points 5 and 6 above), ask a trusted friend to pray over you (and vice versa), or find a prayer partner from your group and commit to praying for one another in these areas.

5 Rs

Thank the Holy Spirit for being with you. Ask God's Spirit to guide your time, help you discern his voice, and assist you in tuning your awareness to God's presence. Then:

- **Read** Jonah 2:2-9. Jonah wrote these words while in one of the worst situations of his life. He was running from God and wound up trapped in the belly of a fish. Yet Jonah continued to praise. (Bonus: Read Jonah 1 and Mark 4:35-41 and note the similarities and differences between Jonah's situation and Jesus'. Why are these important? What do they tell us about Jesus?)

- **React.** What are your initial thoughts about this passage? What words, images, or questions come to mind as you read? Jot down the things that cross your mind.

- **Rehearse.** Read the Scriptures again, this time aloud, and note any repeating words or phrases. Pay attention to themes. What might God be saying about himself here?

- **Receive,** asking God what he wants you to hear. Stay quiet, attentive. Listen for his still, small voice. Pay attention for an image, word, verse, or any thought that he brings to mind.

- **Respond** by writing, drawing, or creating a prayer (of lament and hope, if you'd like) based on your reading today.

Chapter 10

Reflection

1. How did you define suffering when you first began to read this book? How do you define it now?

2. How has your experience of struggle drawn you closer to Jesus?

3. What have you learned thus far about lament? How has it been helpful to you?

4. Are you a different person because of your difficult season? In what ways?

5. In what ways do you think God wants you to pour yourself out for others? Who is God asking you to lament for or with?

6. How can you create room for someone else's lament? What steps can you take to begin to voice it?

7. In what ways can you mobilize your church to begin alleviating the suffering of others? How can you mobilize your church community to begin a process of Protest laments?

5 Rs

Thank the Holy Spirit for being with you. Ask God's Spirit to guide your time, help you discern his voice, and assist you in tuning your awareness to God's presence. Then:

- **Read** Psalm 22. This is a song of David, made famous by Jesus on the cross.[8] This psalm reflects a feeling of God's absence. Where is he? Why does he feel so far away? Psalm 22 would remain dark, but pay special attention to verse 24.

  The truth in all of our laments and pain is that God has not hidden his face from us. He is near and listens to our cries for help. Praise his holy name! Take some time to thank Jesus for his lament—his death and resurrection—on your behalf.

- **React**. What are your initial thoughts about this passage? What words, images, or questions come to mind as you read? Jot down the things that cross your mind.

- **Rehearse**. Read the Scriptures again, this time aloud, and note any repeating words or phrases. Pay attention to themes. What might God be saying about himself here?

- **Receive**, asking God what he wants you to hear. Stay quiet, attentive. Listen for his still, small voice. Pay attention for an image, word, verse, or any thought that he brings to mind.

- **Respond** by writing, drawing, or creating a prayer (of lament and hope, if you'd like) based on your reading today.

Chapter 11

Reflection

1. Have you ever watched a community walk through a process of lament? What did they do? What did you learn from their example?

2. Chapter 11 mentions asking God a series of ekah questions in the early days of lament. Over time, God answered all of them, either directly or indirectly, with himself. What about you? Has God answered any of your lament questions? In what ways?

3. Think back on yourself, or on your heart, when you first started this book. How would you describe your difficult season—and your emotions about it—now?

4. How would you describe God's presence during a season of suffering to a friend?

5. In what ways is God giving you hope and courage in your season of struggle?

6. In what ways do you sense God's "withness"?

5 Rs

Thank the Holy Spirit for being with you. Ask God's Spirit to guide your time, help you discern his voice, and assist you in tuning your awareness to God's presence. Then:

- **Read** Lamentations 5 and Revelation 21. As chapter 11 explains, "All laments—from Job's to Jeremiah's, from Hannah's to yours—are answered in the lament-ending love of Jesus. Lament is the up-to-hope journey because it is ultimately the up-to-Jesus journey." In fact, the overarching theme of Lamentations is a mourning of the destruction of the Temple, the downfall of Jerusalem. And yet, the book of Lamentations is not the end of the biblical story. All of Scripture points to the restoration of the True Temple, Jesus Christ himself—raised up, victorious, making all things new. Amen.

- **React.** What are your initial thoughts about these passages? What words, images, or questions come to mind as you read? Jot down the things that cross your mind.

- **Rehearse.** Read the Scriptures again, this time aloud, and note any repeating words or phrases. Pay attention to themes. What might God be saying about himself here?

- **Receive,** asking God what he wants you to hear. Stay quiet, attentive. Listen for his still, small voice. Pay attention for an image, word, verse, or any thought that he brings to mind.

- **Respond** by writing, drawing, or creating a prayer (of lament and hope, if you'd like) based on your reading today.

acknowledgments

My family: A massive thank you to my parents, Larry and Lydia; my in-laws, Pam and Randy; my aunt Gaye and uncle Scott for letting me write about Cameron. And to my sister, Corey—for cheering me on, babysitting my kids, and liking my articles (even if you didn't actually read them). You have all cared for my family in tremendous ways, especially in the early days of my sickness. We are so grateful for your examples of faith in action. And of course, to Kevin and the boys. I dedicated this book to you—because you are my everything and I couldn't do this without you.

Renewal Church: You are the greatest church planters in the entire world. Plus you shared me with other churches and never once complained. When others in our body have lamented, you have risen to the occasion to bear witness to their pain. You have truly been the church. Kevin and I love you.

Caitlyn Carlson: Thank you for your keen editorial eye, for your compassionate guidance, and for doing it all as a mom of two little ones. You are the real Wonder Woman.

NavPress: Don Pape, David Zimmerman, Melissa Myers, Stephanie Wright, and Elizabeth Symm. It's hard to express this adequately, but you are more than a publishing house. You are a family that I feel grateful to have been adopted into.

Tyndale: Jeff Rustemeyer, Robin Bermel, David Geeslin,

Whitney Harrison. I love the relationship between NavPress and Tyndale—such a beautiful marriage. Plus, you created the most beautiful book cover in the world. Thank you so much for all of your work.

Catherine McNiel: This book would not be possible if it weren't for you, dear friend, looking me straight in the eyes and saying, "Umm . . . I think you need to go to the hospital." You were the first person who gave me permission to stop ignoring my physical pain. You are not only a good neighbor, you are an incredible writer who helped me with inspiration and movie dates—although not nearly as many as we wanted. Why do we have to be adults?

Mitchel Lee, Pam Sampson, and Ashley Egler: Thank you for adding your laments and your experiences of lament to this book. Your voices are such a gift. *You* are such a gift.

My Propel master's cohort: To every woman in my Wheaton College graduate program, seriously, you bless me, amaze me, inspire me, and educate me every day. I love learning with and from you.

The unstoppable team at Propel Women and especially Chris Caine: Thank you for letting me and my writing be a little part of your awesome organization—which truly propels women into all that God has for them. I am grateful to you.

Christina Walker: You are a gift, a healer, a bringer of God's presence. As you know, you have the spiritual gift of making me cry.

Redbud Writers Guild and my Redbud manuscript group: Thank you for reading, editing, and laughing about my overuse of the "be" verb.

Ma' Girls—Jenn, Amanda, Kathy, Hollie: The gift of your friendship is one of my greatest treasures. Here's to many more years of yoga in the mountains and rickshaw rides through downtowns. And to one of my oldest and dearest, Tara, for the amazing photo of the garden of Gethsemane, which gave me this book's ending.

Shannon Ethridge: My writing mentor, the first woman who really believed in me as a writer and taught me to BLAST off. Thank you for writing the foreword and for being *you*.

Heidi Mitchell / D.C. Jacobson: In a world of changing publishing dynamics, you kept on. Thank you for cheerleading this project.

And a special thanks to David and Louise Decker of Deer Ridge Ministries, who gave me a gorgeous Sabbath space to rest and edit this manuscript. Deer actually grazed in front of me while I wrote. It was a writer's paradise.

notes

CHAPTER 1: WHEN YOUR GAME IS CHANGED

1. Online Etymology Dictionary, s.v. "accept," accessed July 2017, https://www.etymonline.com/search?q=accept&source=ds.
2. C. S. Lewis, in a letter to Rev. Peter Bide, April 29, 1959.
3. William Shakespeare, *King Lear,* act 5, scene 3, lines 329–30 from *The Complete Works of Shakespeare*, ed. David Bevington (New York: Longman, 1997), 1218.
4. Bono, "I Still Haven't Found What I'm Looking For," *The Joshua Tree* © 1987 Island Records.
5. Judges 6:12-13.
6. Judges 6:18.

CHAPTER 2: IT'S OKAY TO BE HONEST

1. Claus Westermann, "The Role of the Lament in the Theology of the Old Testament," translated by Richard N. Soulen, *Interpretation: A Journal of Bible and Theology* 28, no. 1 (January 1974): 27.
2. Genesis 4:10.
3. Genesis 1:31.
4. Westermann, "Role of the Lament," 20–21.
5. *Strong's Concordance*, s.v. "yada," accessed July 9, 2018, http://biblehub.com/hebrew/3045.htm.
6. Exodus 15:1-2, 20-21.
7. Walter Brueggemann, "The Costly Loss of Lament," *Journal for the Study of the Old Testament* 11, no. 36 (October 1986): 62.
8. Amos 5:16-17, MSG.
9. Isaiah 6:8.
10. Thomas Watson, *All Things for Good*, first published as *A Divine Cordial*, 1663, (repr: Edinburgh, UK: The Banner of Truth Trust, 2017), 44.
11. Matthew 26:38-39.

CHAPTER 3: BEGIN WITH HOW

1. Janet O. Hagberg and Robert A. Guelich, *The Critical Journey: Stages in the Life of Faith*, 2nd ed. (Salem, WI: Sheffield, 2005), 94.
2. Lamentations 3:28-29, MSG.
3. "Why Is Jeremiah Called the 'Weeping Prophet'?" Bible Study Tools, accessed August 6, 2018, https://www.biblestudytools.com/video/why-is -jeremiah-called-the-weeping-prophet.html.
4. Soong-Chan Rah, *Prophetic Lament: A Call for Justice in Troubled Times* (Downers Grove, IL: IVP Books, 2015), 111. If you're interested in the structure of Lamentations, Rah has an entire chapter (chapter 8) dedicated to its acrostic structure.
5. *Strong's Concordance*, s.v. "ekoh or ekah," accessed July 9, 2018, http:// biblehub.com/hebrew/351a.htm.
6. *A Reader's Hebrew-English Lexicon of the Old Testament*, s.v. "Ekah" (Grand Rapids, MI: Zondervan, 2013).
7. Lamentations 1:1.
8. Hagberg and Guelich, *Critical Journey*, 107. Emphasis in original.
9. Psalm 66:9.

CHAPTER 4: THE GRIEF OF LOVE

1. I first wrote about Cameron and love leaving a mark for *The MOPS Magazine*, "Love Leaves a Mark," Fall 2017. This article is also available here: https://blog.mops.org/love-leaves-a-mark/.
2. Nicholas Wolterstorff, *Lament for a Son* (Grand Rapids, MI: Eerdmans, 1987), 74.
3. Rah, *Prophetic Lament*, 56.
4. This quote is mostly associated with Charles Spurgeon, although an article by Christian George of the Spurgeon Center says it was inspired by another pastor who was inspired, himself, by a Spurgeon sermon: "6 Quotes Spurgeon Didn't Say," *The Spurgeon Center* (blog), August 8, 2017, https://www.spurgeon.org/resource-library/blog-entries/6-quotes -spurgeon-didnt-say.
5. 2 Samuel 1:25-26.
6. Herbert Kretzmer, "Empty Chairs at Empty Tables," *Les Misérables* (Santa Monica, CA: The David Geffen Company, 1987).
7. N. T. Wright, *The Day the Revolution Began: Reconsidering the Meaning of Jesus's Crucifixion* (New York: HarperOne, 2016), 368. Emphasis in original.

CHAPTER 5: HITTING WALLS IN LAMENT

1. Oswald Chambers, "Receiving Yourself in the Fires of Sorrow," Utmost .org, June 25, 2017, http://utmost.org/receiving-yourself-in-the-fires -of-sorrow/.

2. Jeffrey Eugenides, *The Marriage Plot* (New York: Farrar, Straus & Giroux, 2011), 108.
3. Gordon D. Fee and Douglas Stuart, *How to Read the Bible Book by Book: A Guided Tour* (Grand Rapids, MI: Zondervan, 2002), 167.
4. Westermann, "Role of the Lament," 30.
5. Claus Westermann, *Praise and Lament in the Psalms* (Atlanta: John Knox Press, 1981), 271.
6. Song of Songs 2:11-13.

CHAPTER 6: WE CARRY EACH OTHER HOME
1. R. Tuck, "The Relations of Edom and Israel," BibleHub, accessed August 7, 2018, https://biblehub.com/sermons/auth/tuck/the_relations_of_edom_and_israel.htm.
2. The Free Dictionary, s.v. "imprecate," accessed July 11, 2018, https://www.thefreedictionary.com/imprecator.
3. William Shakespeare, *Romeo and Juliet* (Philadelphia: J. B. Lippincott & Co., 1913), 159.
4. Kyle Benson, "The Anger Iceberg," The Gottman Institute, November 8, 2016, accessed August 7, 2018, https://www.gottman.com/blog/the-anger-iceberg/.
5. Some of this content was first featured on JenPollockMichel.com, "Muckily-Dirtily Things," November 25, 2016, http://jenpollockmichel.com/2016/11/25/muckily-dirtily-things-guest-post-by-aubrey-sampson/ (link no longer active). Used with permission.
6. Some of this content was first featured in *More to Life Magazine*, "We Bring Each Other Home," July 1, 2017, https://mtlmagazine.com/article/we-bring-each-other-home/. Used with permission.
7. Anne Lamott, *Stitches: A Handbook on Meaning, Hope and Repair* (New York: Riverhead Books, 2013), 46.

CHAPTER 7: WHEN PAIN IS CHRONIC
1. J. Kevin Butcher, *Choose and Choose Again: The Brave Act of Returning to God's Love* (Colorado Springs: NavPress, 2016), 139.
2. Westermann, "Role of the Lament," 22.
3. Some of this content was first featured on *The MOPS Blog*, "Health in Moments: Embracing Motherhood with an Autoimmune Disease," May 12, 2016, https://blog.mops.org/health-in-moments/. Used with permission.
4. Leslie Leyland Fields, *Crossing the Waters: Following Jesus through the Storms, the Fish, the Doubt, and the Seas* (Colorado Springs: NavPress, 2016), 189. Emphasis in original.

CHAPTER 8: LEARNING TO SAY "YET"
1. My mom often quotes Kay Arthur from *Lord, I Want to Know You* (Colorado Springs: WaterBrook, 2000), 29.
2. C. S. Lewis, *A Grief Observed* (New York: Bantam, 1976), 53–54.
3. Michael Card, *A Sacred Sorrow: Reaching Out to God in the Lost Language of Lament* (Colorado Springs: NavPress, 2005), 109.
4. Card, *Sacred Sorrow*, 109.
5. Timothy Keller, *Walking with God through Pain and Suffering* (New York: Riverhead, 2013), 248–49.

CHAPTER 9: WHEN YOU JUST NEED TO DO SOMETHING
1. See Jonah 1:6.
2. See, for example, Psalm 29:10, Psalm 33:7, and Psalm 89:9.
3. Online Etymology Dictionary, s.v. "rehearse," accessed August 7, 2018, https://www.etymonline.com/word/rehearse.
4. This practice is based on some work of Dr. Rick Richardson, one of my favorite professors.
5. Rick Richardson, *Experiencing Healing Prayer: How God Turns Our Hurts into Wholeness* (Downers Grove, IL: IVP, 2005), 36. Emphasis in original.
6. Richardson says that "if you do not feed your heart with nourishing images of the good, the true, the beautiful and the holy, you will let it be inhabited by images that feed the crooked, the deceptive, the self-serving and the lustful. No other option is open. Jesus needs to be Lord of our imagination!" (65).

CHAPTER 10: BEYOND YOURSELF
1. "Tisha B'Av," Judaism 101, accessed August 7, 2018, http://www.jewfaq.org/holidayd.htm.
2. Card, *Sacred Sorrow*, 120.
3. Rah, *Prophetic Lament*, 99.
4. Card, *Sacred Sorrow*, 29. Emphasis in original.
5. John M. Perkins, *Beyond Charity: The Call to Christian Community Development* (Grand Rapids, MI: Baker Books, 1993), 39.
6. To learn more about Be the Bridge, visit: https://beabridgebuilder.com/about/.
7. Philippians 1:29.
8. *Won't You Be My Neighbor?*, directed by Morgan Neville (New York: Focus Features, 2018).
9. Desmond M. Tutu and Mpho A. Tutu, *Made for Goodness: And Why This Makes All the Difference*, ed. Douglas C. Abrams (New York: HarperOne, 2010), 108.

CHAPTER 11: WHAT KIND OF GOD DO WE HAVE?
1. Nell Bang-Jensen, "Name Post: A List for Zambia," *Names across Nations* (blog), April 7, 2012, http://namesacrossnations.blogspot.com/2012/04

/name-post-list-for-zambia.html. (Note: Mapalo is misspelled in this source.)

2. "Bemba," Encyclopedia.com, accessed August 7, 2018, https://www .encyclopedia.com/humanities/encyclopedias-almanacs-transcripts-and -maps/bemba-0.

3. Aubrey Travis Sampson, "Adding to the Women of Valor Conversation," August 29, 2012, http://www.aubreysampson.com/adding-to-the-women -of-valor-conversation/.

4. Matthew 26:39, KJV.

5. Oxford Living Dictionaries, s.v. "despair," accessed July 13, 2018, https:// en.oxforddictionaries.com/definition/despair.

6. Author Marva J. Dawn poses a similar question in *Truly the Community: Romans 12 and How to Be the Church* (Grand Rapids, MI: Eerdmans, 1992), 52.

7. Online Etymology Dictionary, s.v. "theodicy," accessed July 13, 2018, https://www.etymonline.com/word/theodicy.

8. Lee Strobel, "Why Does God Allow Tragedy and Suffering?" *Christianity Today*, July 22, 2012, https://www.christianitytoday.com/pastors/2012 /july-online-only/doesgodallowtragedy.html.

9. James 5:13-16.

10. "What's in the Name? Chipulukusu Transforms to Mapalo Township," *Zambia Business Times*, July 22, 2017, https://zambiabusinesstimes.com /2017/07/22/whats-in-the-name-chipulukusu-transforms-to-mapalo -township/.

STUDY GUIDE: YOUR LAMENT JOURNEY

1. "Introduction to Job," the Bible App by Life.Church (accessed November 17, 2017).

2. Online Etymology Dictionary, s.v. "rehearse," accessed August 7, 2018, https://www.etymonline.com/word/rehearse.

3. Willis J. Beecher, "Korahites; Sons of Korah," *International Standard Bible Encyclopedia*, accessed September 19, 2018, https://www.biblestudytools .com/encyclopedias/isbe/korahites-sons-of-korah.html.

4. Card, *Sacred Sorrow*, 174.

5. Genesis 15:1-21.

6. Genesis 9:1-17.

7. Will Kynes, "God's Grace in the Old Testament: Considering the *Hesed* of the Lord," *Knowing & Doing*, Summer 2010, http://www.cslewisinstitute .org/webfm_send/430.

8. See, for example, Matthew 27:46.

THE NAVIGATORS® STORY

T HANK YOU for picking up this NavPress book! I hope it has been a blessing to you.

NavPress is a ministry of The Navigators. The Navigators began in the 1930s, when a young California lumberyard worker named Dawson Trotman was impacted by basic discipleship principles and felt called to teach those principles to others. He saw this mission as an echo of 2 Timothy 2:2: "And the things you have heard me say in the presence of many witnesses entrust to reliable people who will also be qualified to teach others" (NIV).

In 1933, Trotman and his friends began discipling members of the US Navy. By the end of World War II, thousands of men on ships and bases around the world were learning the principles of spiritual multiplication by the intentional, person-to-person teaching of God's Word.

After World War II, The Navigators expanded its relational ministry to include college campuses; local churches; the Glen Eyrie Conference Center and Eagle Lake Camps in Colorado Springs, Colorado; and neighborhood and citywide initiatives across the country and around the world.

Today, with more than 2,600 US staff members—and local ministries in more than 100 countries—The Navigators continues the transformational process of making disciples who make more disciples, advancing the Kingdom of God in a world that desperately needs the hope and salvation of Jesus Christ and the encouragement to grow deeper in relationship with Him.

NAVPRESS was created in 1975 to advance the calling of The Navigators by bringing biblically rooted and culturally relevant products to people who want to know and love Christ more deeply. In January 2014, NavPress entered an alliance with Tyndale House Publishers to strengthen and better position our rich content for the future. Through *THE MESSAGE* Bible and other resources, NavPress seeks to bring positive spiritual movement to people's lives.

If you're interested in learning more or becoming involved with The Navigators, go to www.navigators.org. For more discipleship content from The Navigators and NavPress authors, visit www.thedisciplemaker.org. May God bless you in your walk with Him!

Sincerely,

DON PAPE
VP/PUBLISHER, NAVPRESS

www.navpress.com

CP1308